NEW REVISED
CAMBRIDGE GED PROGRAM

Exercise Book
for the
Writing Skills Test

Part Two

D1456396

CAMBRIDGE Adult Education
Prentice Hall Regents, Englewood Cliffs, NJ 07632

Pre-press Production: **TopDesk Pre-Press, Inc.**
Acquisitions Editor: **Mark Moscowitz**
Production Editor: **Shirley Hinkamp**
Interior Design: **LCI Designs**
Cover Design: **Mike Fender**
Prepress Buyer: **Ray Keating**
Manufacturing Buyer: **Lori Bulwin**

ISBN   0-13-601204-3

Prentice-Hall International (UK) Limited, *London*
Prentice-Hall of Australia Pty. Limited, *Sydney*
Prentice-Hall Canada, Inc., *Toronto*
Prentice-Hall Hispanoamericana, S.A., *Mexico*
Prentice-Hall of India Private Limited, *New Delhi*
Prentice-Hall of Japan, Inc., *Tokyo*
Simon & Schuster Asia Pte. Ltd., *Singapore*
Editora Prentice-Hall do Brasil, Ltda., *Rio de Janeiro*

New Revised Cambridge GED Program

Executive Editor
Mark Moskowitz

Writers
Beverly Ann Chin
Gloria Levine
Karen Wunderman
Stella Sands
Michael Ross
Alan Hines
Donald Gerstein

Project Director
Robert McIlwaine

Consultants/Reviewers
Marjorie Jacobs
Cecily Bodnar
Diane Hardison
Dr. Margaret Tinzmann
Nora Chomitz
Bert C. Honigman
Sylvester Pues

Development Editor
Julie Scardiglia

Photo Researchers
Page Poore
Ellen Gratkowsky

Electronic Design
Molly Pike Riccardi

Contents

Introduction

This *Exercise Book for the Writing Skills Test, Part Two* can help you prepare for the essay that makes up Part II of the GED's Writing Skills Test. You can use it along with either the *New Revised Cambridge GED Program: Comprehensive Book* or the *New Revised Cambridge GED Program: Writing Skills*.

The Three Sections of this Book

There are three main sections in this book: Instruction and Exercise, Practice, and Simulation. The three sections share a common purpose—to help you develop the skills you need to be successful with the Writing Skills Test of the GED. The following parts of this introduction describe what you will find in each of the sections in this book and explain how to use them.

The Instruction and Exercise Section

What is the Instruction and Exercise Section? The Instruction and Exercise section of this book is divided into chapters and lessons parallel to those that make up Unit II in either the *New Revised Cambridge GED Program: Comprehensive Book* or the *New Revised Cambridge GED Program: Writing Skills*. This book's lessons both supplement and reinforce those in the Unit IIs. They supplement by instructing about and providing practice in more basic skills than are covered in either *Cambridge GED Program*. They reinforce by building up to end-of-lesson activities as challenging as those in both Programs' Unit IIs.

How to Use the Instruction and Exercise Section. The Instruction and Exercise section of this book can be used alone or together with Unit II in either related *Cambridge GED Program*. In either case, you should work through this book in order from front to back. If you use this exercise book together with one of the related texts, you have a choice. You can work through a lesson in this book and then use the textbook's lesson as a review. Or, you can work through a textbook lesson and use the related lesson in this book for help with points the textbook covers in less detail.

The Practice Section

What Are the Practice Tests? This book has two practice tests that are like Part II of the GED's Writing Skills Test. For each test you are assigned a composition of about 200 words on a GED-like topic. When you take the tests, you should allow yourself no more than 45 minutes for each in order to practice under GED-like conditions.

How to Use the Practice Tests. You should take the Practice Tests after you have completed the Instruction and Exercise section in this book and in Unit II of the *Cambridge GED Program*. You may want to take the Practice Tests in this book after you complete the Practice section in either textbook.

The Simulation Section

What Is the Simulated Test? The Simulated Test is as much like the actual GED Writing Skills Test as possible. It has two parts and the same number of items as the real test. Taking the Simulated Test will help you determine how ready you are to take the GED Writing Skills Test.

How to Use the Simulated Test. You can take the Simulated Test before or after you've taken the Simulated Test in either *Cambridge GED Program*. Take the Simulated Test under the same conditions you will have when you take the real Writing Skills Test of the GED: Work without interruption and do not talk to anyone or consult other materials. You should complete Part I in 75 minutes and Part II in 45 minutes.

Scoring Your Work and Using Your Scores

You will find the Answers and Explanations section at the back of this book to be a useful study tool. The section contains answers to all the direct questions that are asked in the lesson activities in the Instruction and Exercise section of the book. It also has scoring guides and model essays to help you score the essays you write for the Practice Tests. It has answers and explanations for every item in Part I of the Simulated Test and a scoring guide for Part II. After you check your answers to the items on one of the three tests, you can complete the appropriate Performance Analysis Chart. The charts can help you determine which writing skills are your strongest and direct you to parts of the Cambridge programs where you can review topics you need to.

Note: This book requires you to do original writing. There are no entries in the Answers and Explanations section for some of the writing you will do. It would be a good idea to have a teacher or someone else react to your original writing. Others' reactions can help you plan improvements you can make when you do your next original writing.

CHAPTER 1
Daily Writing

Objective

In this chapter you will read about and practice

- fastwriting
- personal writing
- journal writing

Lesson 1

Introduction to Personal Writing

If you are like a lot of people, the idea of writing a 200-word essay on the GED is a little frightening. A technique known as fastwriting can help you overcome your fears.

How can fastwriting help?

- You may be worried that you cannot write fast enough to finish a 200-word essay in the time allowed.

    Fastwriting will show you that you can write 200 words in a very short time—probably in just a few minutes.

- You may wonder whether you will have enough ideas to write a good essay.

    Fastwriting will help you overcome writer's block, the inability to get something down on paper. The fastwriting technique requires that you write. It doesn't matter *what* you write. You can write the same thing over and over if you want to. When you do fastwriting, even if at first you have trouble getting ideas, you will soon find that ideas come to you easily.

- Like many people, you may just freeze up at the very idea of writing.

    When your fastwriting exercises show you that you *can* write a lot of words in a very short time and that you *can* get enough ideas to keep writing for several minutes, you will begin to feel more comfortable with the idea of writing.

How is fastwriting done?

There are very few rules for fastwriting:

> **Rules for Fastwriting**
> 1. Choose a topic to write about.
> 2. Decide how many minutes you will write.
> 3. Time yourself.
> 4. Start writing, and don't stop until the time is up.

Don't concern yourself about the ideas you put down. If you wander off the subject, it doesn't matter. Don't take time to think about the spelling or punctuation of a word. Just keep writing: write anything that comes to mind.

How does fastwriting look?

Two different people decided to write for one minute about their hobbies. Here's what each person wrote:

Fastwriting A

Knitting is my favorite pass time. I knit a lot in winter it helps the evenings to pass quickly. I even knit when I watching television. Some shows you don't have to keep your eyes on the TV all the time.

Time written: ____1____ minute(s)

Words written: ____41____ words

Fastwriting B

I would rather go fishing than do anything else. I like to go by myself. It's the only time I have to be alone with myself. I don't even care if I catch any fish or not. Being out in the open with no one else around helps me to calm down and to think about things in a relaxed manner.

Time written: ____1____ minute(s)

Words written: ____60____ words

Both writers started out writing about a particular hobby. Both of them also wandered away from their original topics a little. The fastwriting about knitting ends up talking about watching television without looking at the screen. The fastwriting about fishing wanders to the emotional benefits of spending time alone in the outdoors. It doesn't matter that the writers wandered off their topics. They continued to write.

The "knitting" fastwriting has usage, sentence structure, and mechanical errors. They don't matter at all. The "fishing" fastwriting is longer than the other one. Length is not important. *The only important thing* is that the writers picked a topic, started writing, and didn't stop until the time was up.

Lesson 1 Activity

Twelve fastwriting exercises follow. Each of the first three is a one-minute exercise. Beginning with the fourth one, each is one minute longer than the one before it.

Over the next few days, complete at least ten of these fastwriting exercises. You may wish to do the first three fastwritings on the lines provided. Remember to record the length of time and the number of words for each fastwriting. As you do these fastwriting exercises, you will find that you can write more and more words per minute and that ideas come more and more easily.

1. Write for one minute about your hobby or what you like to do to relax.

_____

_____

_____

_____

_____

_____

_____

2. Write for one minute about a member of your family.

Time written: _____ **minute(s)**
Words written: _____ **words**

_____

_____

_____

_____

_____

_____

_____

Time written: _____ **minute(s)**
Words written: _____ **words**

3. Write for one minute about a job you have liked or would like to have.

_____

_____

_____

_____

_____

_____

_____

Time written: _____ minute(s)

Words written: _____ words

4. Write for two minutes about your favorite sport or form of exercise.
5. Write for three minutes about your feelings about taking tests.
6. Write for four minutes about why you are studying for the GED.
7. Write for five minutes about a vacation you would like to take.
8. Write for six minutes about your neighborhood or neighbors.
9. Write for seven minutes about your favorite holiday.
10. Write for eight minutes about something someone did that made you very happy.
11. Write for nine minutes about how you would be affected by winning a lot of money.
12. Write for ten minutes about friendship or about what it is that makes a certain person your friend.

There is no entry in Answers and Explanations for this activity. As long as you wrote each fastwriting exercise for the amount of time assigned, without stopping, you have completed this activity perfectly.

Developing a Personal Writing Plan

To Do Today

-Clean blinds
-Change washer-kitchen sink
-Hang clock
-Patch hole-bathroom wall
-Write essay for class
-Do math homework

Menu

Mon.—beans and rice, salad
Tues.—meatloaf, rice, peas
Wed.—chicken, potatoes, corn
Thurs.—spaghetti (use meatloaf)
Fri.—fish cakes, spinach, garlic bread

Spent

groceries $79.89
gas $20.00
socks $18.50

Mrs. Dawson:

Carl will miss the first two hours of school tomorrow because of a medical appointment.

Ralph Toomer
January 17

Fastwriting helps increase your writing speed and makes you feel more comfortable when you write. There are other informal writing activities you can do every day that will help you in other ways to prepare for the essay on the GED.

When you write an essay, your purpose is to make your ideas about a subject clear to a reader. Informal writing that has the purpose of communicating—either with yourself or with someone else—is another step in preparing to write essays. You probably do some writing like that already. While you are preparing for the GED, it would be a good idea to communicate in writing—either with yourself or someone else—every day.

You may make chores lists to remind yourself what you have to do when you get the time. You may find other kinds of lists useful: lists of people's birthdays, shopping lists, menus, and so on. Some people keep lists of all the money they spend to monitor their spending and help in budget planning. You can probably think of other types of lists you would find useful in your daily life—especially lists about things you are likely to forget.

Notes and letters communicate with others: notes to children's teachers, to delivery route drivers, to family members; letters to friends, businesses, government representatives, newspapers, and manufacturers. Perhaps there is someone with whom you could reestablish contact by writing a letter or a note.

The thing to keep chiefly in mind when you write lists, notes, letters—even when you fill out forms—is that you are writing to communicate with yourself or with someone else. Try to express your thoughts as clearly as possible so that the message gets across.

Lesson 2 Activity

Each day from now until you take the GED, make it a point to do some personal writing. Do *useful* writing: a list you will use, a note you will send to or leave for someone, or a letter. Look for opportunities to communicate in writing. The more frequently you write, the easier it gets. All the personal writing you do helps you prepare for the GED.

Following are some suggestions for personal writing you can do.

- Keep a *To Do Today* list each day.
- Begin a *To Do* list for big projects you want to start soon.
- Make a list of phone numbers you need frequently, and put it by the telephone.
- Keep a supermarket shopping list in a convenient spot in the kitchen; when you use something up, write it on the list.
- Keep a pocket-size notebook with you in which you record all your expenses.
- Keep your checkbook register up to date; fill it in completely so you always know how much you have in your account.
- When you take a phone call for someone else, leave a note for that person near the telephone.
- On a calendar write in the names of people to whom you want to remember to send a card.
- When ideas occur to you about something you can write about in your journal (see the next lesson), jot them down in a pocket-size notebook you carry with you.
- When you have strong feelings about a public issue, write to your local newspaper or an elected official.
- Write a note or letter to a friend or relative even if that person lives nearby.
- If you read about an interesting coming event in the newspaper, make a note so you won't forget to attend.
- If you want to remember to ask a question or contribute an idea in class, make a note to remind yourself about that.

There is no entry in Answers and Explanations for this activity. If your daily writing communicates what you want it to, you have completed this activity perfectly.

Many people keep journals or diaries. There are several benefits to keeping a journal. The greatest immediate benefit you could experience now would be the help it would give you in preparing to write the essay for the GED. (There will be further comments about that later in this lesson.)

There are different ways to go about keeping a journal. Some people like to use a diary they buy in a store. Some diaries have small, dated spaces for writing a few lines each day. Entries in small diaries look something like this:

APRIL 4	1993	APRIL 7
Sunday	Cool. Rainy. Mom & Dad came for dinner—turkey. Kids had egg hunt. Jason fell off bike.	
Monday	Didn't go to work because Jason's knee infected. Doctor treated. Kids out of school all week. Charlotte came over.	
Tuesday	Went to work. Mrs. Stroud improving. GED class: Got a 5 on my essay! Feel tired.	
Wednesday	Jason's knee improved. Slept late—sore throat. Made turkey soup. Called Charlotte.	

Such journals are good for making brief notes about events in your life. Reading them again years later can bring a flood of memories.

Some diaries available in stationery stores provide full pages for daily entries, like this one:

SUNDAY, APRIL 4, 1993 (EASTER)

Today was one of the best Easters we've ever had. No one was sick. (Usually someone is still getting over the last of a winter cold.) The children all looked cute in their matching light green suits and dresses—and not one of them fell or spilled anything on their clothes. Mom and Dad came for dinner. We had turkey with all the trimmings. I got up about 6:00 to get the turkey going: George even got up—a little later—and helped me with the meal. Then he went and hid the eggs we dyed last night for the Easter egg hunt. The kids were so excited trying to find the eggs. There was just one little spat when nearly all the eggs had been found (There were 24) and little Lilly hadn't found even one. I was so proud of Charles—without anyone seeing him, he re-hid three of his eggs and then helped Lilly find them. That's going to be a generous man when he grows up!

Many people, however, prefer to use blank notebooks so that they may write as little or as much as they want. If you decide to keep a journal in a blank notebook, it's a good idea to date each entry. You may want to add other details at the beginning of your entry as well: the time, the weather, your location. An example of a journal written in a notebook follows.

Sunday, April 4, 1993 8:30 A.M. Warm already. Home. Easter. Today looks like it's going to be a good day for Easter. The news said that in other parts of the country the weather is cool and rainy. I'm glad to be here. I like Easter to have good weather. I've got a big day ahead of me—but I'm glad I don't have to do any cooking. The whole family is getting together at Shirley's for an outdoor meal—the first one since last fall. Something about the change in the weather and the coming of summer makes me feel the kind of excitement I felt as a child when summer vacation was coming. I have a difficult time concentrating on things. My energy level gets high and I have a hard time sitting still. (My boss has commented on that, unfortunately.) Sometimes I feel like a giddy child in an adult body...

Keeping a journal is different from fastwriting and personal writing (lists, notes, and letters) in a few ways. When you write in a journal, you will probably spend time thinking and planning what to say before each new paragraph or sentence. That kind of planning is a skill you will need to apply when you write the GED essay.

Because you can write whatever you want in a journal, you can write down your opinions about issues. That would be good practice for the GED essay since the topic you write on may require you to express and defend an opinion.

Fastwriting, personal writing, and journal writing are three good activities to prepare for the GED essay. Each has its own benefits; you will probably find it useful to do all three kinds of writing frequently as you prepare for the GED.

Lesson 3 Activity

Purchase or set aside a book (a diary or a notebook) to use for your journal writing. Make a commitment to write in your journal every day; even if you just make a short entry, you will have lived up to your commitment. Write about things that occur in your life or thoughts and feelings that you have.

Some suggestions of things you can write about in your journal follow. Write about

- Members of your family, their lives and interests, your feelings about them, conversations you have with them, things they do
- People with whom you work or take classes, your feelings about them
- Your neighborhood, the people who live there, how it is changing, its relationship to the rest of the city or town where you live
- Your hopes, expectations, disappointments, discouragements, angers, joys, sadnesses, fears, embarrassments, proud moments, successes, victories, loves, spiritual interests
- Conversations you have with other people, stories people tell you, observations you make about other people
- A story you make up
- Your natural environment, changes in the weather and how they affect you and your activities
- Current events in your town or state, in the country or in the world, and your opinions about those events
- Holidays you celebrate and your feelings about them
- Opinions you have, things you like or dislike, things you approve of or disapprove of
- Plans you have for your future, hopes you have for the future of your friends and family members
- Things you come to understand, new knowledge you acquire
- Your childhood, both the pleasant and the unpleasant memories you have
- A problem you are having

There is no entry in Answers and Explanations for this activity. If you fulfill the commitment you make to yourself to write in your journal every day, you have completed this activity perfectly.

CHAPTER 2
The Writing Process

Objective

In this chapter you will read about and practice

- a five-stage writing process
- understanding essay topic assignments
- writing point-of-view statements
- brainstorming
- clustering
- organizing notes
- mapping
- writing paragraphs
- writing essays
- revising essays
- editing essays

Lesson 1 — Introduction to Writing as a Process

The fastwriting, personal writing, and journal writing you have been doing are helpful preparation for essay writing. Fastwriting helps you build writing speed and gain confidence in your ability to come up with ideas to write about. Personal writing helps you increase your ability to express your thoughts clearly. Journal writing requires that you think and plan before you write. It also gives you the opportunity to write about your opinions. The GED essay calls on all the skills you build by fastwriting, personal writing, and journal writing.

Essay writing is different in some ways from the kinds of writing you have been practicing, however. Essays are usually more formal and more carefully organized. The *right* way to do fastwriting—to write as soon as an idea pops into your head—is the *wrong* way to write an essay. A better way to write an essay is to follow a five-stage process that allows you to plan, write, and polish an essay in an orderly fashion.

The writing process is similar to other processes you use all the time in your daily life, for example, food shopping. Before you even go to the supermarket, you think about what you need. Next you write a list. If you are really efficient you will organize your list according to the sections at the market: produce, dairy, baked goods, etc.

The following paragraphs show the steps for writing an essay.

Before you write an essay, you decide what to write about. Then you write down everything that comes to mind about the subject. This is called brainstorming: making notes about things to say in an essay. You may divide your list into categories or organize your notes so that related ideas are grouped together.

Now you are ready to write your essay, making sure to put related ideas into paragraphs. You check to be sure that it has all the ideas and only the ideas that should be in it.

Last you make sure your ideas are carefully presented in sentences that are grammatically and mechanically correct.

The next six lessons are about the writing process. In them you will read about and practice the things you should do at each stage of the process.

Lesson 1 Activity

Write a brief description of the process you now follow when you write an essay on an assigned topic. (If you took a Writing Skills Predictor Test in one of the other Cambridge GED books, you may describe the procedure you followed when you wrote the essay.)

How many of these steps do you follow when you write an essay?

Step 1: Thinking of ideas to write about and making notes about them

Step 2: Organizing the notes so that related ideas are grouped

Step 3: Writing a draft of the essay in four or more paragraphs

Step 4: Checking the essay and making changes so that only ideas that should be in the essay are included and they are presented in a logical, effective manner

Step 5: Correcting any errors in the presentation of the ideas: errors in grammar, sentence structure, spelling, capitalization, and punctuation

There is no entry in Answers and Explanations for this activity. The purpose of the activity is to have you think about how you now write essays and to compare your current method to the one you will concentrate on in the next six lessons.

Lesson 2 — Understanding Essay Topics

In Part II of the Writing Skills Test, you will be given 45 minutes to write a 200-word essay on an assigned topic. The topic will ask you to give your opinion or an explanation of a particular situation. The situation will be one with which most adults are familiar. The essay you write has to be on the assigned topic; you cannot write on a topic of your own choosing. However, you may write anything you want about the assigned topic—as long as you stick to that topic. There is no right or wrong "answer" to the essay assignment. The directions will ask what *you* think about a certain situation. Whatever *you* think about that situation is what you should write.

When you come to Part II of the Writing Skills Test, you should spend a few minutes reading, rereading, and thinking about the assigned topic. That will be time well spent because if you end up writing an essay that is *off* topic, your essay will be given *no score at all*.

Key Words in Topics

Read *every* word in the GED essay topic you are assigned. Take note of words that seem especially important. Reread the topic once or twice to be sure you understand all of its implications. If you skip or ignore a word or two, you might write an essay that is off topic. Consider the difference in meaning between these two sentences:

A. One judge makes first-offense drunk drivers place bumper stickers on their cars that identify them as convicted drunk drivers.

B. One judge makes drunk drivers place bumper stickers on their cars that identify them as convicted drunk drivers.

Sentence A tells how a judge punishes *first-offense* drunk drivers. Sentence B talks about a judge's punishment for drunk drivers in general. Because *first-offense* is missing from Sentence B, the punishment must apply to *all* drunk drivers, first offenders and repeat offenders. That difference in meaning is very important.

Suppose you had to write an essay to give your opinion of the punishment in Sentence A. If you ignored the *first-offense* part of the sentence, you might write an essay that is on the wrong topic. You might include a sentence like this:

> However, I think a person who is convicted of drunk driving again and again deserves a punishment more severe than a bumper sticker.

That sentence would not be appropriate in an essay about the punishment in Sentence A. All the ideas in an essay giving an opinion about the punishment in Sentence A should be about the punishment *only* as it applies to *first offenders*, not as it might apply to repeat offenders. Repeat offenders are not mentioned or implied in Sentence A. That same sentence could work in an essay about the punishment in Sentence B, however, because that punishment is for all drunk drivers.

Study the following example topic, which is similar to a GED essay topic. Then read the discussion and answer the question that follows the topic.

EXAMPLE TOPIC 1

Many employers now offer alternatives to the traditional workweek schedule. Some of those alternatives are working part time, working flexible hours, and working at home without a fixed schedule.

What kind of workweek schedule would you choose for yourself if you could? Write a composition of about 200 words explaining why you would like the workweek schedule you would choose. Provide reasons and examples to support your explanation.

An essay on that topic should be about the writer's choice of a *workweek schedule* for *himself* or *herself*.

Imagine that you read five essays written in response to that topic. You find the following sentences, one in each of the essays. Judging by the content of each sentence, which of the essays would you think were on topic, and which would you think were off topic?

ESSAY 1   I am usually more alert in the evening than I am in the morning, so working at home on a schedule I set for myself would allow me to be most productive.

ESSAY 2   I also think that people should be able to trade jobs with each other on a rotating basis so that no one gets bored doing the same thing all the time.

ESSAY 3	I would choose a flexible work schedule. It would afford me the opportunity to be more involved with raising my child.
ESSAY 4	Most people waste a lot of the time they spend at work, anyway, so it would be best to find out how much time they waste and dock their pay.
ESSAY 5	Besides, there wouldn't be any way to tell if people put in all the hours they're paid for if everybody worked at home.

A writer should do three things in an essay on the topic:

- Describe the workweek schedule he or she would choose
- Give reasons for the choice of a workweek schedule
- Give examples that support the choice of a workweek schedule

Sentences about anything else would not be appropriate and could make the essay wander off topic. Therefore, Essays 1 and 3 are probably on the assigned topic because the sentences from both essays give *reasons* the writers like particular kinds of work schedules. Essay 2 is probably off topic: the sentence from that essay is about rotating job assignments, *not* about work schedules. The sentences from Essays 4 and 5 are about monitoring *other people's* work habits: those essays are probably off topic.

The Two Parts of Topic Assignments

The essay topic assignment on the GED has two parts, just like Example Topic 1. The first part provides a little background on the subject of the essay. In Example Topic 1, for instance, you read about alternative workweek schedules. The second part of a topic assignment tells you what to write about the subject. That part contains important directions. Sometimes, as in Example Topic 1, there is a direct question. If there is a question, it is to help you focus on the subject and what you should write about it.

In the second part of Example Topic 1, you learn four things:

- How long the composition should be (about 200 words)
- What you are to write about (the alternative workweek schedule you would choose and why you would like it)
- That you should include reasons
- That you should provide examples

Look at another topic. Example Topic 2 is a little different from Example Topic 1.

EXAMPLE TOPIC 2

Credit cards have changed Americans' spending habits. The use of credit cards has benefited some Americans and caused problems for others.

Explain how using credit cards can be beneficial or problematic, or both. Write a composition of about 200 words to present your views. Provide reasons and examples to support your opinions.

From the first part of the topic, the background, you can tell that the subject of the essay will be credit cards. As in Example Topic 1, the second part says to write a composition of about 200 words. The directions then give a choice: an essay can be about (1) how credit cards can be *beneficial*, (2) how credit cards can be *problematic*, or (3) how credit cards can be both *beneficial* and *problematic*.

Both example topics offer choices. In the first, the writer can choose the kind of work-week schedule to write about; in the second, the writer decides whether to write about benefits, problems, or both. GED essay topic assignments offer similar kinds of choices.

Stating Your Point of View

Because GED essay topic assignments provide choices, you need to decide what point of view to express or position to take in your composition. As soon as you understand what the topic requires, you should state your position on the subject. It helps to think of a point of view as an answer to a question someone has asked you.

Example Topic 2 follows, printed this time with key words underlined. There is no question in the second part of the topic assignment, but you can make up a question using some of the key words from the topic.

EXAMPLE TOPIC 2

<u>Credit cards</u> have changed <u>Americans' spending habits</u>. The use of credit cards has <u>benefited</u> some Americans and <u>caused problems</u> for others.

<u>Explain how using credit cards</u> can be <u>beneficial</u> or <u>problematic</u>, or <u>both</u>. Write a composition of about 200 words to present your views. Provide reasons and examples to support your opinion.

A question that can be made using some of the underlined key words is this:

Is the <u>use</u> of <u>credit cards beneficial</u> or <u>problematic</u>— or <u>both</u>—for <u>Americans</u>?

To decide on the point of view to take in an essay, write the answer to the question. Three possible answers follow as examples:

Using credit cards is beneficial for most Americans.
Using credit cards creates problems for some Americans.
Using credit cards is both beneficial and problematic to American consumers.

The sentence you write to state your point of view is not necessarily the sentence you would use as the first one in your composition, although it could be. More than anything, the statement you write is for your own benefit. You can read and reread your point-of-view statement while you think of ideas to include in your essay. (Generating ideas will be covered in the next lesson.) The essay you write will explain and support your point of view.

Lesson 2 Activity

Read the following topic. Answer questions 1 to 3 about the topic. Follow the directions in item 4: they will help you state a point of view about the topic. Save the point-of-view statement you write. You will use it again in the next step in the writing process.

TOPIC

In 1900 American youths were not required to attend high school—and few did. Today, laws require students to stay in school until they are 16 years old or older.

Do you think young people should be required to attend school until they are in their late teens? Write a composition of about 200 words explaining your answer to this question. Give reasons and examples to support your view.

---

1. Which of the two parts of the essay topic assignment gives some background about the subject of the composition?

_____

2. What is the subject of the composition to be?

_____

3. What does the essay topic assignment say should be written about the subject?

_____

4. **(a)** Underline key words in the topic assignment.
    (b) Write a question using some of the key words you have underlined.
    (The answer to the question will be a point-of-view statement.)

    _____

    _____

    (c) Write the answer to the question in (b). This sentence will state the point of view for a composition.

    _____

    _____

    Check your answers on page 91.

For Further Practice

Two essay topic assignments follow. Answer Questions 1–3 and follow the directions in Item 4 in the lesson activity as related to Topic 1 and Topic 2. Discuss your answers with your teacher or another person.

TOPIC 1

Many companies run youth employment projects that hire teenagers for summer or year-round work in exchange for wages or high school credit—or both. The teenagers are usually paid relatively low wages for the jobs they do, but they gain valuable work experience and make important contacts for the future.

Do you think such employment projects benefit or take advantage of teenagers, or both? Write a composition of about 200 words explaining your point of view on this question. Give reasons or examples to support your opinion.

TOPIC 2

Many people have strong feelings about owning pets. Some think the pleasures and benefits of having a pet are too important to miss. Others will have nothing to do with a pet of any kind.

What are your feelings about owning a pet? Write a composition of about 200 words explaining whether you think having a pet is desirable or undesirable. Provide reasons and examples to support your view.

Generating Ideas

In the last lesson you concentrated on understanding essay topic assignments and on writing sentences that state a point of view. When you know what point of view you will write about, you can take the first step in the writing process. In that step you spend time thinking of and making notes about ideas to put in your essay.

This lesson will show you two different ways to make notes about the ideas that come to you when you are planning a composition. One of the ways is called **brainstorming**; the other is called **clustering.**

Brainstorming

When you brainstorm, you let ideas occur while you think about a word, a phrase, or the statement of an essay's point of view. You make notes about every idea that comes to you.

Brainstorming is similar to fastwriting in three ways: you write quickly, you write *anything* that comes to mind, and you don't worry about spelling, grammar or punctuation. Brainstorming is also different from fastwriting: when you brainstorm, you do *not* make notes in sentences. Writing in sentences takes too long. Rather, just write down words or short phrases that will remind you later about what you thought of.

It is important to write *everything* that crosses your mind even if you think a certain idea seems unimportant or ridiculous. You never know where one thought might lead you. Any thought could be the most important one you have.

Brainstorming notes look a bit like some shopping lists. An example follows. These notes were written by a married woman who was thinking about the word *home*.

home					
house	green	yard	trees	swing set	
family	husband/father		children	Ted and Carrie	school
meals	sing	popcorn	argue		
cooking	washing	cleaning	warm	secure	happy

She wrote "home" at the top of the page. Then she wrote, in order, other words that occurred to her. Some of the words she wrote must have occurred to her when she was thinking about the house she lives in: *house, green, yard, trees, swing set.* Then she began to think of her family. Thoughts of her family led her to think of some things they do together: they share *meals, sing,* eat *popcorn,* and *argue.* She then began to think of chores she and her husband must do at home: *cooking, washing,* and *cleaning.* Finally, she thought about the qualities of her home: *warm, secure,* and *happy.* At some point she thought of the word *school.* Even though it doesn't seem to fit, she wrote it because she thought of it.

If the woman uses the notes to write a paragraph about her home, she may decide not to include all her ideas in the paragraph. She may decide not to write about the physical appearance of her house at all.

Before you continue with this lesson, try doing a little brainstorming yourself. Practice by spending at least one minute writing all the things that come to your mind as *you* think about the word *home*. Or, you might like to use another word to brainstorm about. Use one of the following words, or any word you like:

children	drugs	friend	GED	holiday
job	mother	school	sickness	television

Use this space to brainstorm for one minute or more on whatever word you like. Write the word on the line at the top of the space. Try to write ten or twenty words.

_____

You may wish to use separate sheets of paper to practice brainstorming on other words.

Clustering

Clustering is another form of brainstorming. The thinking process you use is the same, but the way you make notes is different. If the woman who brainstormed on the word *home* had used the cluster method, she might have made notes that looked like this:

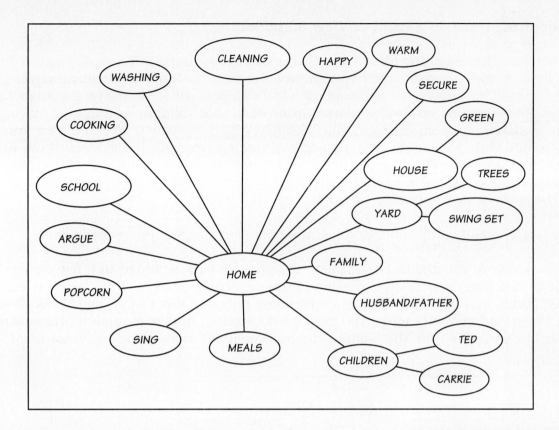

The word on which the brainstorming is done goes in the middle of the page, and a circle is drawn around it. Related words that come to mind are written around the central word. They, too, are circled, and a line is drawn to join words, creating clusters of related ideas. Here, *green* extends from *house* because the house is green; *trees* and *swing set* extend from *yard* because they are in the yard; the children's names extend from *children*.

A cluster (or any brainstorm) should not take a lot of time: write as fast as you can. Don't waste time making notes neat.

Try doing a cluster yourself. Use the space below to do your first cluster. It might be a good idea to use a different word from the one(s) you used earlier in this lesson. Write the word you want to think about in the circle in the middle of the space that follows. Then draw extensions and write words as you think of them. Spend at least a minute thinking and noting your ideas down in a cluster.

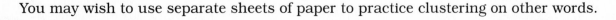

You may wish to use separate sheets of paper to practice clustering on other words.

Generating Ideas on a Point-of-View Statement

When you are generating ideas for a GED essay, you will be thinking about the point-of-view statement you wrote after you studied the topic assignment. Remember that you will be writing your essay for someone else to read; you will be explaining your point of view so that someone else will understand it. Keep that thought in mind as you brainstorm; it may help ideas come to you. It might also help you to pretend that you are going to talk with a friend about your point of view on the assigned subject. What would you imagine saying to your friend?

Here is an example of a cluster on a point of view about Example Topic 2 (see page 16). The point of view is this:

The use of credit cards benefits some Americans and causes others problems.

In the circle in the middle of the page, the point of view is stated in a few words. The brainstormed ideas appear on extensions from the center circle.

It is usually not possible to make notes using only one word when you think about a point of view on an essay topic. You may need to write phrases in such a brainstorm or cluster. As you look over the sample cluster, you'll see that there are ideas about the

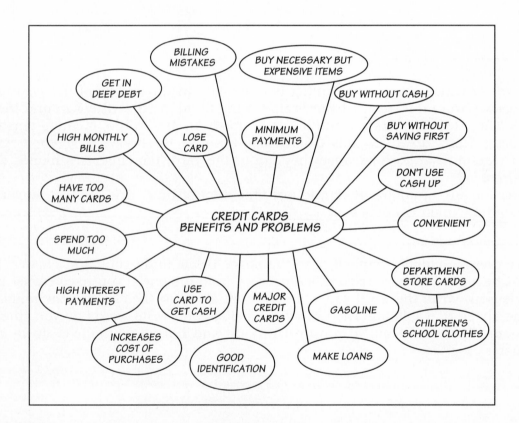

benefits of the use of credit cards. (Most of those ideas are on the right side of the cluster.) There are also ideas about the problems with credit cards. (Most of those ideas are on the left side of the cluster.) The point of view for the essay requires discussion of both benefits and problems.

In the next lesson you will read about and practice grouping and organizing ideas you have generated and made notes about.

Lesson 3 Activity

Look back at your answer to 4(c) in the Lesson 2 Activity on page 18. Brainstorm on that point of view. Spend from 3 to 5 minutes thinking about the point of view. Write your notes in a cluster in the space provided here. Write quickly; put down *all* the ideas that come to mind. Do *not* write in sentences: write in words or short phrases. When you have finished, save your cluster. You will need to use it in the next lesson activity.

There is no entry in Answers and Explanations for this activity. Discuss your cluster with your teacher or another person.

For Further Practice

Topics 3 and 4 follow. For each topic assignment,

(a) underline key words.

(b) write a question using some of those key words.

(c) write the answer to that question, which is the point of view for a composition.

(d) brainstorm on the point of view, writing your notes in a cluster or list.

TOPIC 3

Many doctors today recommend that adults exercise regularly and vigorously to improve their health and prolong their lives. Other doctors express concern that people are exercising too much or in ways that are harmful rather than helpful.

What is your opinion of the value of regular, vigorous exercise? Write a composition of about 200 words explaining whether you think such exercise is beneficial or harmful. Provide reasons and examples to support your opinion.

TOPIC 4

We are living in a time when casual or unprotected sex is extremely dangerous. AIDS is a deadly disease rapidly spreading in all communities.

Write a composition of about 200 words explaining what adults can do to protect themselves from the spread of AIDS. Be specific and provide examples, reasons, and details to support your view.

Check your answers on page 91.

Lesson 4

Organizing Ideas

When you brainstorm or cluster on a point of view, you may make ten, twenty, or more notes. You have probably noticed, however, that during brainstorming or clustering, ideas do not occur to you in an organized fashion. Rather, you probably find that you write unrelated notes next to each other. The second step of the writing process is to organize your notes.

One of the characteristics of an effective essay is good organization. Organized notes are the tool for achieving that aspect of an essay's effectiveness. They serve as a map to guide you as you write the paragraphs and sentences that make up your essay.

This lesson will show you ways to organize your brainstorming or clustering notes. It will also show you how to create a map to guide your essay writing.

Organizing Brainstorming Notes

Take another look at the notes about *home* the married woman wrote.

home					
house	green	yard	trees	swing set	
family	husband/father		children	Ted and Carrie	school
meals	sing	popcorn	argue		
cooking	washing	cleaning	warm	secure	happy

It is not easy to see which words or ideas go together, or how they go together. One way to organize them is to rewrite them in labeled lists of related ideas, as follows:

property	family	activities	chores	atmosphere
house	husband/father	meals	cooking	happy
green	Ted	sing	washing	warm
yard	Carrie	popcorn	cleaning	secure
trees		argue		
swing set		games		
garden				

There are some things to notice about these lists:

- Each group has a label. All the words about the house and yard are grouped under "property," for example.
- One of the labels, "family," appeared in the original brainstorm. It is a good label because the people named are all family members.
- Some of the words from the original brainstorm are deleted from the organized list. *School* was deleted because it doesn't relate to the other words; *children* was deleted because the names of the children are in the group labeled "family."
- There are some new words in the organized list that were not in the brainstorm: *garden* and *games*.

When you organize brainstorming or clustering notes, you can remove words that are not useful or add new words. Throughout the steps in the writing process, you can make changes whenever better ideas occur to you.

Just for practice, read over these brainstorming notes based on the word *food*. In the space following them, organize the notes by creating short lists of words that go together. Be sure to label each list.

Food				
orange	peas	beef	beans	apples
carrots	hamburger	potatoes		crab
pineapple	chops	cherry		ham
cheese	sole	trout	cod	

There are a few different ways the food list could be organized. All the foods could be organized in two groups:

<u>Vegetable Foods</u>: orange, peas, beans, apples, carrots, potatoes, pineapple, cherry
<u>Animal Foods</u>: beef, hamburger, crab, chops, ham, cheese, sole, trout, cod

It would also be possible to make four lists that include most of the foods:

<u>Vegetables</u>: peas, beans, carrots, potatoes
<u>Fruit</u>: orange, apples, pineapple, cherry
<u>Meat</u>: beef, hamburger, chops, ham
<u>Fish</u>: crab, sole, trout, cod

If the words are grouped that way, *cheese* does not fit into any group.
You may have organized the foods in one of those two ways, or you may have thought of another way to group them that would be just as logical.

Organizing Clustering Notes

Organizing notes in a cluster takes less time than organizing brainstorming notes: it isn't necessary to rewrite the notes in lists. Rather, after you have decided how to group the notes, you just write the labels in a convenient spot in the cluster and give them a code letter or number. Then, write the code in or near each of the circles in the cluster. An example of organized cluster notes follows.

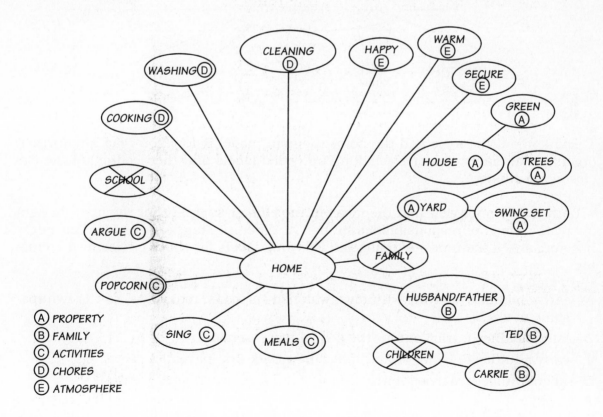

A man was assigned the following topic for an essay:

TOPIC

At some point in your life, you became aware that you no longer thought and acted as a child does but that you had entered a more mature stage of your life.

How did you come to know that you had become an adult? Write a composition of about 200 words explaining your answer to this question. Give specific examples that demonstrate your points.

The man wrote this statement of his point of view:

Point of View: I realized I was an adult when my responsibilities had changed from those of a child to those of an adult.

Then the man made this cluster:

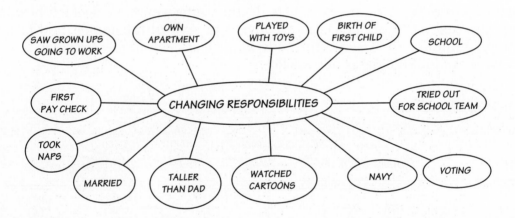

Think about the topic and the notes the man made. Before you read any further, organize the man's cluster by making up coded labels and then coding all the circles in the cluster.

Both the point of view and the ideas in the cluster suggest that the man thought about the kinds of responsibilities he had at different stages in his life. You might have organized his notes by using the following labels for those circles in the cluster:

A—early childhood: playing with toys, watched cartoons, took naps, saw grownups going to work
B—later childhood: tried out for the school team, school
C—early adulthood: voting, Navy, taller than Dad, first paycheck
D—full adulthood: married, birth of first child, own apartment

You may have found a different way to organize the notes. Any organization that is logical would be a good one.

Mapping

After you have labeled the circles in a cluster or grouped the ideas in a brainstorm, you can make a map to guide you as you write a composition.

The map that follows is based on the cluster the man made about the adulthood topic. It is organized by the four life stages labeled *A, B, C,* and *D,* as in the discussion you just read.

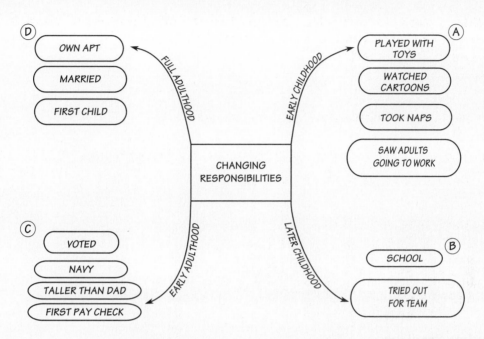

To make a map, write the point of view of the essay, using a short phrase, in a box in the center of a sheet of paper. For each group of ideas in the cluster, draw a line extending from the box. Write one of the labels on each of the extensions. At the ends of the extensions, copy the groups of notes from the cluster. As you copy the notes, you may reword or shorten them to save space and time.

Lesson 4 Activity

For this activity use the cluster you made in the Lesson 3 Activity on page 23.

First, make up coded labels and organize the cluster by coding the circles in it. Then, make a map based on the organized cluster. When you have finished, save your map. You will need to use it in the next lesson activity.

Use the space on the next page to make your map.

There is no entry in Answers and Explanations for this activity. Discuss your map with your teacher or another person.

For Further Practice

Topics 5 and 6 follow. For each topic assignment,

(a) underline key words.

(b) write a question using some of those key words.

(c) write the answer to that question, which is the point of view for a composition.

(d) brainstorm on the point of view, writing your notes in a cluster.

(e) organize the cluster by coding the ideas in it.

(f) make a map based on the organized cluster.

TOPIC 5

Success means different things to different people. Some people regard wealth and material possessions as marks of success. Others think that influence and power indicate success. Still others measure success by the quality of their relationships with friends and family members.

Identify the way you measure success. Write a composition of about 200 words explaining how you measure success. Provide reasons and examples to support your explanation.

TOPIC 6

There are sports for nearly every taste. For those who prefer individual sports, there are golf, jogging, and swimming. Baseball, football, and basketball satisfy many people who prefer team sports.

If you had the choice of participating in an individual or a team sport, which kind would you choose? Write a composition of about 200 words in which you explain why you prefer the type of sport you select. Give reasons and examples to support your opinion.

Check your answers on pages 91–94.

Lesson 5 Writing an Essay

In this third stage of the writing process, you express your ideas about your point of view in sentences. Working from a map, you state and support your views in four or more unified paragraphs that, together, form the draft of your essay.

Like a television story, an essay should have a beginning, a middle, and an end. Within the first few minutes of most television stories, you know what the show will be about. That's the beginning. The story then unfolds. That's the middle. Finally, all the threads that have run through the story come together and the story concludes. That's the end.

Likewise, at the beginning of an essay, you state your point of view. The reader then knows immediately what the essay is about. In the middle of the essay you present the reasons and examples that support your point of view, perhaps using one paragraph for each. Finally, you end the essay with a paragraph that draws the essay's points together into a conclusion.

The building blocks of that essay structure are paragraphs. Each paragraph in an essay has its own important function. The introductory paragraph states your point of view and introduces the major ideas the essay presents. Two or more paragraphs in the middle of the essay are made up of details, examples, and reasons that support the essay's point of view. The concluding paragraph sums up and ends the essay.

In this lesson you will concentrate on writing unified paragraphs, writing the three kinds of paragraphs an essay needs (introductory, middle, and concluding), and writing an essay by following a map.

Analyzing Paragraphs—Topic Sentences

A paragraph is a group of sentences, all of which are about the same topic.

The first word in a paragraph is always indented; that is, it is written about an inch to the right of the margin. When an author introduces a new topic, he or she writes a new paragraph.

In many paragraphs a topic sentence announces the topic of the paragraph. The topic sentence is in italic print in the following paragraph. What is the topic of the paragraph?

New car prices have gone up steadily since the 1930s. In the thirties many new cars cost only $500. By 1960 new car prices were up to about $3,000. Today you will pay $10,000 or more for the average new car.

The topic sentence lets you know that the topic of the paragraph is new car costs and how they have changed since the thirties. The next three sentences give examples that demonstrate how costs have risen over time.

Look at the two paragraphs on the left below. Neither of them has a topic sentence. Which two sentences from the three at the right would be a good topic sentences for the paragraphs?

Paragraphs

Teenagers who used their incomes for entertainment once made up the largest group of minimum-wage earners. Now many people who can earn only the minimum wage support whole families.

Since 1938, when it was established, the amount of the minimum wage has risen. Coverage has been extended to include many types of workers the original law did not protect.

Sentences

The purpose of the minimum wage has changed since 1938.

The characteristics of the minimum-wage earner have changed.

The amount and coverage of the minimum wage have changed over time.

The second sentence would be the best topic sentence for the first paragraph. It says that minimum-wage-earner characteristics have changed. The paragraph compares two types of minimum-wage earner to demonstrate the change.

The third sentence—the one about the changes in the amount and coverage of the minimum wage—would be the best as the topic sentence of the second paragraph, which gives some details about those changes.

Neither of the two paragraphs says that the *purpose* of the minimum wage has changed. That rules the first sentence out as a topic sentence because it talks about a change in purpose.

Analyzing Paragraphs—Supporting Sentences

Because all the sentences in a good paragraph are about the same topic, the supporting sentences in a paragraph give details, examples, or reasons that support the idea in the topic sentence.

The following is not a good paragraph because one of the sentences is off topic. Which sentence should not be in the paragraph?

Some older cameras are difficult to operate. Many older cameras cannot be operated without light meters. Others are hard to focus. A modern camera with a built-in meter and an automatic focus costs about $40.

Since the topic of the paragraph is the *difficulty* of operating some *older* cameras, the last sentence in the paragraph is off topic. It discusses a *modern* camera and its *cost*. Without that last sentence, the paragraph would be unified. No sentence would be off topic.

Is the following paragraph unified?

Not everyone who knows about the dangers of cigarette smoking is a nonsmoker. Many informed people continue to smoke. The price of a pack of cigarettes varies from state to state. Smoking is even increasing among some groups, although they know the hazards.

The paragraph is not unified because the sentence about the price of a pack of cigarettes does not belong in the paragraph. The *price* sentence would make a good topic sentence for a paragraph about varying cigarette prices:

The price of a pack of cigarettes varies from state to state. It is not the cost of the cigarettes, themselves, that differs. The difference is in the amount of tax a state charges on cigarettes. Some states tax cigarettes heavily; other apply only low taxes.

Think about the following two paragraphs. Are they unified paragraphs? If not, which sentence(s) should not be in the paragraphs?

Movie studios do not produce many movies today. They spend their money to make a few high-budget movies. The last movie I saw was too expensive. Studios prefer to finance a few movies that will bring in a high profit rather than several low-profit movies.

Natural events can be as destructive as bombs. Whole cities can be leveled by a volcano or an earthquake. One atom bomb destroyed Hiroshima. A tidal wave can wipe out an entire island.

Neither paragraph is unified. In each paragraph the third sentence would have to be removed for the paragraph to be unified. In the paragraph about movies studios producing only high-profit movies, the sentence about the cost of seeing a particular movie is off topic. In the paragraph about destructive natural events, the sentence about the atom bomb is off topic because a bomb is not a natural event.

Writing Paragraphs—Topic Sentences

Before you write a topic sentence, you should have a clear idea about what the topic and purpose of the paragraph are. Suppose you are going to write a paragraph about how *difficult* it is to be parent. The *topic* of the paragraph is the problems of being a parent. The *purpose* of the paragraph is to list some examples of the problems parents have. With those two things in mind, it is possible to write the topic sentence for the paragraph. The topic sentence would mention the topic (the problems of being a parent), and *imply* the purpose (to list examples of those problems).

Here are two possible topic sentences:

Parents face many problems raising their families.

Bringing up children presents problems to any parent.

Both sentences mention the topic. Both imply the purpose of the paragraph: they lead you to expect that the paragraph will go on to list some of the problems parents have.

Sometimes you may have a clear idea about what the supporting sentences in a paragraph will say but not about the paragraph's topic and purpose. Without a clear notion about the topic and purpose of a paragraph, it is not easy to write a topic sentence. Look at the following supporting sentences. What are their topic and purpose?

Look the car over before you buy it. Have a mechanic check it.
Compare its price to the prices of similar used cars.

Hints about buying used cars is the topic of the paragraph. The purpose is to list three steps to take before buying a used car. A topic sentence for that paragraph should mention the topic and imply the purpose:

There are three things you should do before you buy a used car.

Try writing some topic sentences. The following notes describe the topics and purposes of two different paragraphs. Write topic sentences that would be appropriate.

Topic: Reasons to Get a GED
Purpose: To list three reasons people have for getting a GED

Topic Sentence: _____

_____

Topic: Rising Prices for Necessities
Purpose: To give some examples of climbing prices for necessary items.

Topic Sentence: _____

_____

For the first topic and purpose, a topic sentence might say

People have different reasons for getting a GED.

For the second topic and purpose, you might have written

The prices of many necessary items continuously rise.

The following two paragraphs do not have topic sentences. Think about what their topics and purposes are. Then write a topic sentence for each paragraph.

In Japan the school year is about 240 days long. Japanese students—even first-graders—spend two hours a day doing homework. Many Japanese students attend extra classes to prepare for examinations.

Topic: _____

Purpose: _____

Topic Sentence: _____

_____

A 1987 survey showed that 78% of working people wish they had a different job. Another recent survey reported that 87% of all workers do not like their jobs.

Topic: _____

Purpose: _____

Topic Sentence: _____

_____

The topic of the first paragraph is the amount of time Japanese students devote to school. The purpose is to give three examples of the amount of time Japanese students study. A topic sentence could be

Japanese students spend long hours studying.

The topic of the second paragraph is workers' discontent with their jobs. The purpose is to report the results of the two surveys. A topic sentence could say

Two recent surveys show that most workers are not happy with their jobs.

Writing Paragraphs—Supporting Sentences

The map you make before you begin writing an essay can be especially helpful when you write the supporting sentences in a paragraph. It can serve as the plan you follow to keep from going off topic. It is easy to write a paragraph that is not unified. Each sentence you write can give you new ideas, but those ideas may not belong in your paragraph. If you follow the map you have made, you will write a unified paragraph more easily.

Suppose you are writing a paragraph with the following topic, purpose, and topic sentence:

Topic: My Favorite Kind of TV show
Purpose: To give three reasons I like suspense mysteries.
Topic Sentence: I like suspense mysteries more than anything else on television.

Your map lists three reasons for your TV show preference:

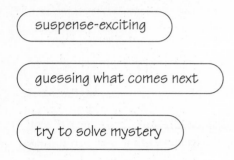

Supporting sentences stating those reasons, together with the topic sentence, will create a unified paragraph:

I like suspense mysteries more than anything else on television. I like the excitement I feel when the suspense has me on the edge of my seat. It is fun to try to figure out what will happen next. I like to try to solve mysteries before the solutions are shown.

The notes in a map are usually brief phrases. When you write a paragraph, you turn those phrases into sentences.

Try writing some supporting sentences. Read the following notes about the topic and purpose of a paragraph and look at the mapped ideas.

Topic: Car Owners' Expenses
Purpose: To list three expenses car owners have.

Now, complete the following paragraph by writing three supporting sentences based on the notes from the map. (The topic sentence is written for you.)

People who own cars have many expenses. _____

_____

_____

_____

_____

_____

There are many ways the three supporting sentences could be written. One way to complete the paragraph is this:

> Most states require car owners to buy costly insurance. Every car owner has to buy gasoline. When repairs are necessary, most car owners have to pay for parts and labor.

Writing Paragraphs—A Summary

The essay-planning steps you take pay off when you begin writing paragraphs. You make a note about your point of view to guide you as you generate ideas by brainstorming or clustering. Knowing that you will be writing paragraphs, you organize your notes by grouping ideas that go together and making a map. The parts of the map serve as outline for the paragraphs you write for the essay.

This is the map you studied in the last lesson.

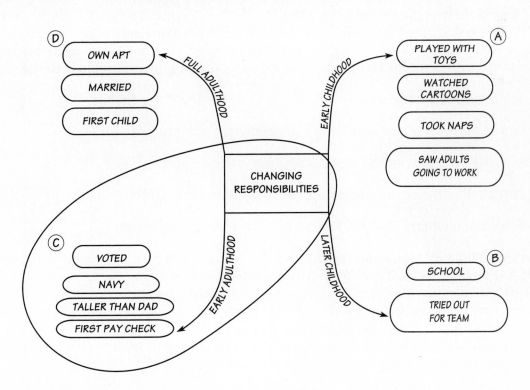

The circled portion of that map will be used to review how a paragraph can be written following the notes in a map.

There are two things you need to have clearly in mind before you can write the topic sentence of a paragraph: (1) the topic of the paragraph and (2) the purpose of the paragraph.

If it helps you, you can make notes on the map about a paragraph's topic and purpose. The following shows how such notes could be written.

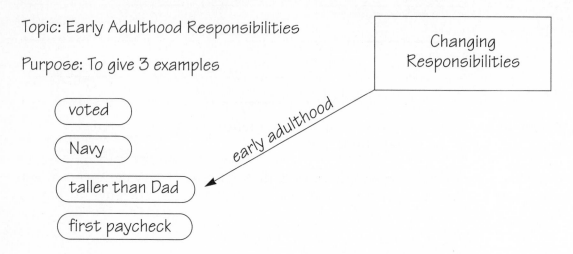

Topic: Early Adulthood Responsibilities

Purpose: To give 3 examples

early adulthood

Changing Responsibilities

voted

Navy

taller than Dad

first paycheck

With those notes as an aid, a topic sentence can be written:

In my late teens, when I had become taller than my father,

I began to have some adult responsibilities.

That topic sentence announces the topic: responsibilities in early adulthood. It implies the purpose of the paragraph: to mention some of those responsibilities. It does the two things a topic sentence should do.

Sometimes it works best to write at least one sentence for each note in a map. The "taller than Dad" note was used in the topic sentence, so at least three more sentences should be written. A draft for the paragraph follows. Notice how it is related to the map.

In my late teens, when I had become taller than my father, I

began to have some adult responsibilities. I got my first job—

working on the counter in a hamburger stand. Soon after I

turned 18 an election came up, so I was able to vote for the

first time. When I was 19, I inlisted in the Navy and began to

realize my childhood was over.

The draft paragraph has one sentence for each note in the map. The sentences describe the events in the writer's early adulthood in chronological order. Notice that the words "first paycheck" from the map were not used in the paragraph, but the words "first job" appear. The paragraph has errors in it, but they can be corrected in the editing stage of the writing process.

Try writing a paragraph. Write another paragraph for the same essay. Pretend that you are the man who made the map. Write the paragraph about full adulthood responsibilities as though you were that man. Use the portion of the map that follows.

You may want to start by making notes on the map about the topic and purpose of the paragraph. Then write the topic sentence. Finally, write the supporting sentences. You can do your writing in the space below the map or on a separate sheet of paper.

own apt.

married

first child

full adulthood

Changing
Responsibilities

_____

_____

_____

_____

_____

_____

_____

_____

_____

_____

_____

There are many ways to write the paragraph. One example follows. Notice that the topic sentence mentions the topic of the paragraph (full adulthood responsibilities) and implies the purpose (to give examples).

By the time I was in my twenties, I had so many adult responsibilities that I knew I was fully an adult. I took an apartment on my own and began paying rent. I got married and moved to a larger, more expensive apartment. My wife and I had a daughter, our most important responsibility.

Using a Map to Write an Essay

At the beginning of this lesson you read that an essay should have a beginning, a middle, and an end. An essay's first paragraph should introduce the whole composition. It should state the thesis, or the point of view, of the composition and should indicate what major points the middle of the essay will cover. One way to introduce an essay is to explain or imply what the structure of the essay is. Therefore, before you begin writing the introduction, you should take a minute to plan the order of the middle paragraphs in the essay.

Consider this map again. The circled part will be especially useful in writing an introductory paragraph. The numbers at the four corners of the map show a plan to write the middle paragraphs in time order.

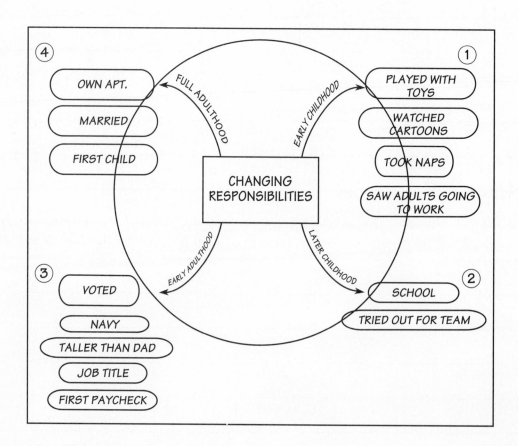

The map outlines a man's responsibilities at four different stages in his life. An introductory paragraph could briefly mention how the man's responsibilities changed over time. It could name some of the life stages.

> I knew I had become an adult when the responsibilities I had was no longer those of a child. My responsibilities was those of an adult. In my childhood I had almost no responsibilities until I started going to school. The quality and number of my responsibilities changed until all my responsibilities were adult ones.

The thesis, or point of view, is presented at the beginning of the introduction. (The thesis answers the question in the second part of the topic assignment: "How did you come to know that you had become an adult?") The other sentences imply that the essay will describe the writer's responsibilities at various stages in his life. The words *child, childhood,* and *adult* all appear in this introductory paragraph. (The errors in the paragraph can be corrected by editing later.)

The map for this essay has four categories. It would be possible, but not necessary, to write four middle paragraphs for the essay. The *later childhood* category is rather small and can be combined with the *early childhood* category so that there is only one paragraph devoted to childhood responsibilities. Here is a draft of the paragraph.

> As a young child my main responsibility was to be a child. I played with toys, watched cartoons on television, and took naps. When I started going to school, I was responsible for being there on time. I also had to do my homework. I tried out for the basketball team and made it.

A final paragraph sums up and ends the essay. Following is a version of a concluding paragraph:

> In my adolescence I thought I would be able to measure my adulthood by the kinds of freedom I had. I realize now that adulthood is measured in responsibilities. With each passing year, I am more an adult.

When you have followed a map to write the beginning, middle, and end paragraphs of an essay, your draft is complete. It may be revised and edited in the last two stages of the writing process.

Lesson 5 Activity

For this activity use the map you made in the Lesson 4 Activity. Using the following lines, write a draft essay based on the map. Think carefully about the topic and purpose for each of the middle paragraphs and the concluding paragraph. When you have finished, save your draft. You will revise it in the activity at the end of the next lesson.

_____

_____

_____

_____

_____

_____

_____

_____

_____

_____

_____

_____

_____

_____

_____

_____

_____

_____

_____

_____

_____

_____

_____

_____

_____

_____

_____

_____

_____

_____

_____

_____

_____

_____

_____

_____

_____

_____

_____

_____

_____

_____

_____

_____

_____

_____

_____

_____

_____

There is no entry in Answers and Explanations for this activity. Discuss your essay with your teacher or another person.

For Further Practice

Topics 7 and 8 follow. For each topic assignment

(a) underline key words.

(b) write a question using some of those key words.

(c) write the answer to that question, which is your point of view.

(d) brainstorm on the point of view, writing your notes in a cluster.

(e) organize the cluster by labeling and coding the ideas in it.

(f) make a map based on the organized cluster.

(g) write a draft of an essay based on the map.

TOPIC 7

Movie ratings are intended to help people decide what movies to see or to allow their children to see. Television listings often provide warnings about the content of programs for the same purposes.

How do ratings or warnings affect your decisions about your own or your children's movie or television watching? Write a composition of about 200 words in which you explain your answer to this question. Provide reasons and examples in your explanation.

TOPIC 8

There are many factors that contribute to job satisfaction: challenge, schedule, location, pay, benefits, opportunity, atmosphere, and others.

Describe the factors that are most important to you in making a job satisfying or unsatisfying. Write a composition of about 200 words explaining how important the factors you choose are for job satisfaction. Provide reasons and examples to support your opinions.

Lesson
6

Revising an Essay

When you are drafting your essay, you concentrate on translating the notes on your map into paragraphs. While you are writing, you cannot stand back to look at the whole essay. When you have finished the draft, however, you should reread it from beginning to end with a critical eye. You will probably find things you want to improve. You should make whatever changes you think will enhance your essay's effectiveness.

In this lesson you will concentrate on things to look for when you revise by studying examples of revisions made in the draft of the adulthood essay. Take a moment to read through the complete draft of the essay, which follows.

I knew I had become an adult when the responsibilities I had was no longer those of a child. My responsibilities was those of an adult. In my childhood I had almost no responsibilities until I started going to school. The quality and number of my responsibilities changed until all my responsibilities were adult ones.

As a young child my main responsibility was to be a child. I played with toys, watched cartoons on television, and took naps. When I started going to school, I was responsible for being there on time. I also had to do my homework. I tried out for the basketball team and made it.

In my late teens, when I had become taller than my father, I began to have some adult responsibilities. I got my first job— working on the counter in a hamburger stand. Soon after I turned 18 an election came up, so I was able to vote for the first time. When I was 19, I inlisted in the Navy and began to realize my childhood was over.

By the time I was in my twenties, I had so many adult responsibilities that I knew I was fully an adult. I took an apartment on my own and began paying rent. I got married and moved to a larger, more expensive apartment. My wife and I had a daughter, our most important responsibility.

In my adolescence I thought I would be able to measure my adulthood by the kinds of freedom I had. I realize now that adulthood is measured in responsibilities. With each passing year, I am more an adult.

When you revise an essay, you should look critically at four things:

- Point of view
- The content
- The organization
- The conclusion or summary

Point of View

When you think about the point of view or central idea in your essay, ask yourself this question:

Is your opinion or point of view clearly stated in one sentence?

The central idea should be so clearly stated that a reader could not misunderstand what your essay is about. It is best to state the central idea in one sentence.

In the adulthood essay, the central point is not clear because it is not stated in one sentence. The following revision corrects that problem:

I knew I had become an adult when the responsibilities I had
                                                          but
was no longer those of a child. ~~My responsibilities~~ those of an
                                                          ∧
adult.

Before the revision, the first sentence said that simply putting away childish responsibilities was the sign of adulthood. That sentence was misleading because it told only half the story. The revision makes it clear that it was the *change* in types of responsibility that caused the awareness of having reached adulthood.

Content

When you think about content, you consider the *middle* of your essay: the two or more paragraphs that discuss the reasons or examples that support the essay's point of view. Ask yourself these questions:

1. Do the examples, details, and reasons support the point of view?
2. Are the examples, details, and reasons specific?
3. Is it clear how they support the central idea?

In the adulthood essay, the three middle paragraphs describe the specific types of responsibilities the man had at three different periods of his life. It is clear that the writer's intent is to show how the type of responsibilities he had gradually changed as he grew older.

In the last sentence in the second paragraph, however, it is not clear how making the basketball team illustrates a kind of responsibility. It can be improved as follows:

> became a member of   gained new responsibilities:
> I ~~tried out for~~ the basketball team and ~~made it.~~
>   attending practices and games.

The revision ties the sentence into the central idea.

Organization

You should be able to answer *Yes* to these questions if your essay is well organized:

1. Is the point of view stated at the beginning?
2. Are there two or three supporting ideas that are clearly stated?
3. Are there words and phrases that show how the supporting ideas relate to the central idea?

The adulthood essay's point of view is in the first sentence. Its three supporting paragraphs are clear. In all of the paragraphs, there are words and phrases that link the supporting ideas to the point of view. However, in the third paragraph, the first sentence contains some words that do not help relate the paragraph to the central idea: *when I had become taller than my father.* The paragraph is about certain responsibilities as symbols of early adulthood: working, voting, and joining the Navy. Even though a son's height could be a symbol of adulthood, this essay is about responsibility as a sign of adulthood. The comment about height, therefore, should be left out:

> In my late teens, ~~when I had become taller than my father,~~
>
> I began to have some adult responsibilities.

Now it is clearer that the paragraph is about adult responsibilities.

Conclusion or Summary

A summary should restate an essay's point of view; a conclusion should follow logically from everything that is said in an essay.

The summary of the adulthood essay is not good because it brings in an idea that is not mentioned anywhere else in the essay: freedom. This summary might make a good ending for a different essay, but it is not appropriate for this essay. A more appropriate summary— one that summarizes *this* essay's points—should be written:

> ~~In my adolescence I thought I would be able to measure my~~
>
> ~~adulthood by the kinds of freedom I had. I realize now that~~
>   The nature of my   changes
> ~~adulthood is measured in~~ responsibilities. With each passing
>   When the responsibilities I had were like those of
> year. ~~I am more~~ an adult, I knew I had become an adult myself.

Now the conclusion summarizes the three middle paragraphs of the essay and restates the central point. The essay is now ready for the final stage editing: making changes in grammar, punctuation, capitalization, and spelling.

Lesson 6 Activity

For this activity, use the draft essay you wrote in the Lesson 5 Activity on page 42. Read through your draft critically. Ask yourself questions about its point of view, content, organization, and conclusion or summary. Revise the draft, making any changes you think will improve it. When you have finished revising your draft, save it. You will edit it in the next lesson.

There is no entry in Answers and Explanations for this activity. Discuss your revisions with your teacher or another person.

For Further Practice

Topics 9 and 10 follow. For each topic assignment

(a) underline key words.
(b) write a question using some of those key words.
(c) write an answer to that question, which is your point of view.
(d) brainstorm on the point of view, writing your notes in a cluster.
(e) organize the cluster by labeling and coding the ideas in it.
(f) make a map based on the organized cluster.
(g) write a draft of an essay based on the map.
(h) revise the draft.

TOPIC 9

Most people experience difficult periods during their lives. At such times they need the support of family and friends.

Explain how family members and friends can support a person who is having temporary difficulty of some sort. Write a composition of about 200 words to explain your opinion on this subject. Be specific and provide examples and reasons to support your opinion.

TOPIC 10

Volunteers make it possible for small service agencies to reach people who need assistance of some kind. However, some people argue that volunteers who are not professionally trained are usually more of a liability than a benefit to service agencies.

Explain your opinion about the value of volunteers in service agencies. Write a composition of about 200 words in which you provide reasons and examples to support your opinion.

Editing an Essay

A revised draft is nearly a finished product. Editing adds the polish and turns the draft into a final essay. Editing improves the way ideas are expressed. When you edit, you make the essay read smoothly. You look at each sentence separately in the context of its paragraph and correct any errors or slips of the pen you find. There are four questions to ask as you reread the draft:

- Do the sentences flow smoothly, or should some of them be shortened or combined?
- Are the sentences grammatically correct?
- Are the sentences structurally acceptable?
- Are there mechanical (spelling, punctuation, or capitalization) errors?

Later in this lesson you will see how the adulthood essay can be edited. First, however, take a look at a few ways to improve the flow of sentences.

Sentence Flow—Shortening Sentences

Usually sentences should state thoughts briefly. When you are editing, you may notice a sentence with too many words. Look at the following sentence as an example:

> The two sisters who lived across the street lived above the store that
> sold antiques.

That sentence can be shortened:

> The two sisters lived above the antique store across the street.

The shortened sentence is clearer and keeps all the important information. It uses eleven words instead of the fifteen words in the original.
This sentence is too long:

> The score of the football game was 43–14 as the Forty-Niners beat the
> New York Giants in a hard-fought game.

It can be shortened:

> The Forty-Niners beat the New York Giants 43–14 in a hard-fought game.

Practice shortening sentences. Write a shorter version of each of the sentences on page 50.

The weeds grew very fast reaching about three feet tall in just about three days.

_____

_____

The reason he did not want to go to the show was that he does not like movies that are about detectives and that have a lot of violence in them.

_____

_____

Writing an essay can be fun if you know how to go about it the best way and if you go about it that way.

_____

_____

The life of an army recruit is a tough life and it requires obedience to the sergeant who drills you and discipline.

_____

_____

The store is up the hill two blocks away and the little girl is heading there to buy some candy.

_____

_____

The candidate was smiling and waving and was talking to his supporters on his way to the platform.

_____

_____

There are a few ways to shorten each sentence. The following sentences show to shorten each sentence above by eliminating unnecessary words.

The weeds quickly grew to about three feet tall in three days.

He did not want to go to the show because he does not like violent detective movies.

Writing an essay can be fun if you go about it in the best way.

An army recruit's life is tough and requires obedience to your drill-sergeant and discipline.

The little girl is heading to the store two blocks up the hill to buy some candy.

The candidate was smiling, waving, and talking to his supporters on his way to the platform.

Sentence Flow—Combining Sentences

Combining sentences can make your thoughts flow more evenly. Combining two short sentences helps to vary the lengths of your sentences so that their rhythms do not become boring. This series of short sentences becomes boring:

The boy likes cats. He has cat for a pet. His cat is a tabby. His cat plays with toys. The toys are shaped like mice.

Here is a way to combine those sentences:

The boy likes cats and keeps a pet tabby that plays with mouse-shaped toys.

Combine the sentences in the following pairs:

The crowd was cheering. They were excited because the football game was suspenseful.

_____

_____

Those men work in the steel mill. The mill employs most of the men in this town.

_____

_____

Sam has a new car. To try it out, he sped down Highway 9.

_____

_____

Mary enjoys reading mysteries. She reads three or four mysteries at a time.

_____

_____

They like to go to the movies. They especially like going on Saturday nights.

_____

_____

There are several ways to combine those pairs of sentences. The following demonstrates one way for each.

The excited crowd was cheering because the football game was suspenseful.

Those men work in the steel mill, which employs most of the men in this town.

To try out his new car, Sam sped down Highway 9.

Mary enjoys mysteries so much that she reads three or four at a time.

They like to go to the movies, especially on Saturday nights.

Sentence Flow—Transition Words

Transition words show how one idea or group of ideas is related to another. They help a reader understand the relationships between sentences or paragraphs. Transition words are always helpful; they are often necessary. Consider this pair of sentences in which there are no transition words:

He didn't eat all day. He was a little depressed.

Those sentences express two related facts. How are they related? Either of the following sentences could report the situation accurately, depending on the circumstances. (The transition words are in italic print.)

He didn't eat all day. _Consequently_, he was a little depressed.

Because he was a little depressed, he didn't eat all day.

In the first version, not eating caused depression; in the second, depression caused a loss of appetite. One or the other may be true, but without a transition word, a reader would have to guess which was the case.

A variety of relationships between ideas and events can be made clear by the use of transition words. The following chart lists transition words often used to make relationships clear.

TRANSITION WORDS

To add ideas

along with	as well as
also	in addition
and	too
another	moreover
besides	furthermore

To compare ideas

as...as	like
just as	likewise
more than	similarly

To contrast ideas

although	nevertheless
as opposed to	on the other
but	hand
despite	still
even though	unless
however	while
in contrast	yet

To conclude

finally	in summary
in conclusion	therefore
in short	in brief
thus	

To introduce an example

for example	one of the
for instance	such as
one kind of	to illustrate

To emphasize an idea

especially	in fact
indeed	most of all
not only ...	that is
but also	

To show time relationships

after	finally	now
at first	following	since
at last	in the meantime	then
at the same time	last	when
at times	meanwhile	while
before	not long after	until
during		

To show cause/effect

as a result	if ... then
because	since
consequently	so
for that reason	therefore
thus	

Rewrite the following sentence groups adding transition words that demonstrate the indicated relationship.

I like football. James like concerts. *(Contrast the ideas.)*

_____

_____

The boss docked their pay. The employees went on strike. *(Show cause/effect.)*

_____

_____

I like movies. I like television. *(Compare the ideas.)*

_____

_____

He was tying his shoe. The lace broke. *(Show the time relationship.)*

_____

_____

She didn't go to work. She didn't call in. *(Emphasize the second idea.)*

_____

_____

Natural disasters are quite destructive. Tornadoes can level whole towns. *(Introduce the example.)*

_____

_____

I like to go to work. I have friends there. I like the satisfaction my job gives me. *(Show cause/effect and add one idea to another.)*

_____

_____

There are several ways to use transition words to show the indicated relationships. One way for each sentence follows.

I like football, but James likes concerts.

The boss docked their pay, so the employees went on strike.

I like movies as much as I like television.

When he was tying his shoe, the lace broke.

Not only did she not go to work, but she also didn't call in.

Natural disasters are quite destructive. For example, tornadoes can level whole towns.

I like to go to work because I have friends there. I also like the satisfaction my job gives me.

Editing a Draft

When you edit a draft, you should do it in stages. The first thing to look at is sentence flow. After that, when all the sentences are in their final form, check the grammar, sentence structure, and mechanics.

Here is the adulthood essay in its revised form. In this lesson, you will see how it can be edited.

I knew I had become an adult when the responsibilities I had
                                                        but
was no longer those of a child. ~~My responsibilities was~~ those of
an adult. In my childhood I had almost no responsibilities until I
started going to school. The quality and number of my responsibilities changed until all my responsibilities were adult ones.

As a young child my main responsibility was to be a child. I
played with toys, watched cartoons on television, and took
naps. When I started going to school, I was responsible for
being there on time. I also had to do my homework. I ~~tried out~~
became a member of   gained new responsibilities: attending
~~for~~ the basketball team and ~~made it~~
                                              practices and games.
In my late teens, ~~when I had become taller than my father,~~
I began to have some adult responsibilities. I got my first job—
working on the counter in a hamburger stand. Soon after I
turned 18 an election came up, so I was able to vote for the
first time. When I was 19, I inlisted in the Navy and began to
realize my childhood was over.

By the time I was in my twenties, I had so many adult
responsibilities that I knew I was fully an adult. I took an apartment on my own and began paying rent. I got married and
moved to a larger, more expensive apartment. My wife and I had
a daughter, our most important responsibility.

~~In my adolescence I thought I would be able to measure my~~
~~adulthood by the kinds of freedom I had. I realize now that~~
The nature of my   changes
~~adulthood is measured in~~ responsibilities . With each passing
When the responsibilities I had were like those of
year. ~~I am more~~ an adult, I knew I had become more an adult
myself.

The first sentence in the essay can be shortened:

> I knew I had become an adult when ~~the~~ ^my^ responsibilities
>
> ~~I had~~ was no longer those of a child. ~~My responsibilities was~~ ^but^
>
> those of an adult.

There is still a grammatical error in the sentence, but that can be corrected in the next stage of editing. For now, at least the sentence is shorter.

Also in the first paragraph, there should be a transition at the beginning of the last sentence to show how it relates to the sentence before it. Another transition word, *finally*, will show that the sentence reports the last point the paragraph makes:

> ^From then on^   ^finally^
>
> ^The quality and number of my responsibilities changed until^
>
> all my responsibilities were adult ones.

In the second paragraph two sentences can be combined:

> When I started going to school, I was responsible for being
>
>   ^and doing^
> there on time, ~~I also had to do~~ my homework.

Three sentences in the fourth paragraph need transition words to show how events relate to each other in time:

> ^When I got out of the Navy,^   ^Two years later,^
>
> I took an apartment on my own and began paying rent. I got
>
>   ^Soon after that^
> married and moved to a larger, more expensive apartment.
>
> My wife and I had a daughter, our most important responsibility.

The last paragraph could be improved by the addition of introductory transitional words:

> ~~In my adolescence I thought I would be able to measure my~~
>
> ^All through my life,^ The nature of my
>
> ~~adulthood by the kinds of freedom I had. I realize now that~~
>
>   ^changes^
> ~~adulthood is measured in~~ responsibilities ^With each passing^
>
> When the responsibilities I had were like those of
>
> year. ~~I am more~~ an adult, I knew I had become an adult myself.

Now the thoughts in the essay and the relationships between them are clear. It is time to read through the essay again, this time looking for grammatical, structural, and mechanical errors. To do this, it is best to read the essay sentence by sentence out loud.

There is a subject–verb agreement problem in the first sentence of the essay. *Responsibilities* takes the plural verb *were*:

> I knew I had become an adult when ~~the~~ ^my^ responsibilities ~~I had~~
>
> ~~was~~ ^were^ no longer those of a child. ~~My responsibilities was~~ ^but^ those of
>
> an adult.

The introductory phrase in the first sentence of the second paragraph should be changed. *As a young child* cannot describe *my main responsibilities*. This change corrects the problem:

> ~~As~~ ^When I was^ a young child, my main responsibility was to be a child.

Note that the change required the addition of a comma because the new introduction to the sentence contains a verb.

In the third paragraph, *enlisted* is misspelled. In addition, a comma is needed after the introductory phrase in the next-to-the-last sentence, which contains a verb, *turned*.

> Soon after I turned 18, an election came up, so I was able
>
> to vote for the first time. When I was 19, I ^e^nlisted in the Navy
>
> and began to realize my childhood was over.

In the final paragraph the verb must be *has changed* rather than *changes* because the sentence describes a process that was going on and that continues.

> ~~In my adolescence I thought I would be able to measure my~~
>
> All through my life, ^T^he nature of my
>
> ~~adulthood by the kinds of freedom I had. I realize now that~~
>
> has change~~s~~^d^
>
> ~~adulthood is measured in~~ responsibilities^.^ ~~With each passing~~
>
> When the responsibilities I had were like those of
>
> year. ~~I am more~~ an adult, I knew I had become an adult myself.

All the serious errors in the essay have been corrected. With the completion of editing, the essay is in its final form. It would be a good idea to read it through one more time from beginning to end as a final check.

The final essay is shown on page 58.

I knew I had become an adult when ~~the~~ my responsibilities ~~I had was~~ were no longer those of a child. ~~My responsibilities was~~ but those of an adult. In my childhood I had almost no responsibilities until I started going to school. From then on The quality and number of my responsibilities changed until finally all my responsibilities were adult ones.

When I was ~~As~~ a young child my main responsibility was to be a child. I played with toys, watched cartoons on television, and took naps. When I started going to school, I was responsible for being there on time. ~~I also had to do~~ and doing my homework. became a member of ~~I tried out for~~ the basketball team and gained new responsibilities: attending ~~made it~~ practices and games.

In my late teens, ~~when I had become taller than my father,~~ I began to have some adult responsibilities. I got my first job—working on the counter in a hamburger stand. Soon after I turned 18, an election came up, so I was able to vote for the first time. When I was 19, I enlisted in the Navy and began to realize my childhood was over.

By the time I was in my twenties, I had so many adult responsibilities that I knew I was fully an adult. When I got out of the Navy, I took an apartment on my own and began paying rent. Two years later, I got married and moved to a larger, more expensive apartment. Soon after that My wife and I had a daughter, our most important responsibility.

~~In my adolescence I thought I would be able to measure my~~ All through my life, The nature of my ~~adulthood by the kinds of freedom I had. I realize now that~~ has changed. ~~adulthood is measured in~~ responsibilities With each passing When the responsibilities I had were like those of year. ~~I am more~~ an adult, I knew I had become an adult myself.

Lesson 7 Activity

For this activity, use the revised draft you worked on in the Lesson 6 Activity on page 48. Edit the draft to bring the essay to its final form. First check to see that the sentences read smoothly; shorten and combine sentences and add transition words. Then correct any grammatical, structural, and mechanical errors. Finally, read your essay through one last time as a final check.

There is no entry in Answers and Explanations for this activity.

For Further Practice

Topics 11 and 12 follow. For each topic assignment

(a) underline key words.
(b) write a question using some of those key words.
(c) write the answer to that question, which is your point of view.
(d) brainstorm on the point of view, writing your notes in a cluster.
(e) organize the cluster by labeling and coding the ideas in it.
(f) make a map based on the organized cluster.
(g) write a draft of an essay based on the map.
(h) revise the draft.
(i) edit the draft.

TOPIC 11

Some people feel that many essential goods and services should be paid for by the government through taxes: electricity, water, natural gas, medicine, and others. Other people think consumers should continue to pay for the goods and services they use.

What is your opinion about the way essential goods and services should be paid for—by the government or at cost to individuals? Write a composition of about 200 words in which you explain your answer to this question. Provide reasons and examples to support your opinion.

TOPIC 12

Some people think handguns should be banned because they are used to commit many violent crimes. Others say that the constitutionally granted right to bear arms, including handguns, is an important one to protect in this day and age.

Do you think handguns should be banned or not? Write a composition of about 200 words in which you explain your opinion about this question. Provide reasons and examples to support your opinion.

CHAPTER 3
Reviewing the Writing Process

Objective

In this chapter you will

- review the writing process
- write essays in 45 minutes

Lesson 1

Practice the Process

Between now and the time you take the GED, practice writing as much as you can. Continue or resume making entries in your journal. (You might use writing in your journal as a warm-up exercise before you write a practice essay.) Continue doing other kinds of writing. Above all, practice writing essays using the steps of the writing process.

In the activity at the end of this lesson, there are fifteen topics for your essay-writing practice. Here are some suggestions about ways to use the list:

- Work through the list in order, writing an essay on each topic.
- First, write essays on the listed topics you like or on the topics you think would be easiest to write about. Later, write essays on the topics you like least or find most challenging.
- Pick a topic at random and write an essay on it.
- Write more than one essay per topic. Defend a different point of view in each or use different examples and reasons in each.

When you practice writing essays, set aside enough time so that you can finish the whole process without interruption. When you are writing your first few essays, time yourself. Start timing when you read the topic and stop when you have finished editing. If it takes you longer than 45 minutes, begin giving yourself less and less time to finish an essay until you are comfortable completing an essay within 45 minutes. (In the next lesson there will be some suggestions about budgeting your time.)

It would be a good idea to get other people to read your essays. Have them comment on how clear and effective your essays are. A teacher or another person may be able to help you see improvements to make in an essay or in your method of writing essays.

The more you practice, the more comfortable you will become with writing essays, and the better you will perform on the GED essay.

Lesson 1 Activity

Fifteen GED-like essay topics follow. Using the suggestions in this lesson and in the next one, write essays on the following topics between now and the time you take the GED.

TOPIC 1

Many companies run youth employment projects that hire teenagers for summer or year-round work in exchange for wages or high school credit—or both. The teenagers are usually paid relatively low wages for the jobs they do, but they gain valuable work experience and make important contacts for the future.

Do you think such employment projects benefit or take advantage of teenagers, or both? Write a composition of about 200 words explaining your point of view on this question. Give reasons or examples to support your opinion.

TOPIC 2

Many people have strong feelings about owning pets. Some think the pleasures and benefits of having a pet are too important to miss. Others will have nothing to do with a pet of any kind.

What are your feelings about owning a pet? Write a composition of about 200 words explaining whether you think having a pet is desirable or undesirable. Provide reasons and examples to support you view.

TOPIC 3

Many doctors today recommend that adults exercise regularly and vigorously to improve their health and prolong their lives. Other doctors express concern that people are exercising too much or in ways that are harmful rather than helpful.

What is your opinion of the value of regular, vigorous exercise? Write a composition of about 200 words explaining whether you think such exercise is beneficial or harmful. Provide reasons and examples to support your opinion.

TOPIC 4

We are living in a time when casual or unprotected sex is extremely dangerous. AIDS is a deadly disease rapidly spreading in all communities.

Write a composition of about 200 words explaining what adults can do to protect themselves from the spread of AIDS. Be specific and provide examples, reasons, and details to support your view.

TOPIC 5

Success means different things to different people. Some people regard wealth and material possessions as marks of success. Others think that influence and power indicate success. Still others measure success by the quality of their relationships with friends and family members.

Identify the way you measure success. Write a composition of about 200 words explaining how you measure success. Provide reasons and examples to support your explanation.

TOPIC 6

There are sports for nearly every taste. For those who prefer individual sports, there are golf, jogging, and swimming. Baseball, football, and basketball satisfy many people who prefer team sports.

If you had the choice of participating in an individual or a team sport, which would you choose? Write a composition of about 200 words in which you explain why you prefer the type of sport you select. Give reasons and examples to support your opinion.

TOPIC 7

Movie ratings are intended to help people decide what movies to see or to allow their children to see. Television listings often provide warnings about the content of programs for the same purposes.

How do ratings or warnings affect your decisions about your own or your children's movie or television watching? Write a composition of about 200 words in which you explain your answer to this question. Provide reasons and examples in your explanation.

TOPIC 8

There are many factors that contribute to job satisfaction: challenge, schedule, location, pay, benefits, opportunity, atmosphere, and others.

Describe the factors that are most important to you in making a job satisfying or unsatisfying. Write a composition of about 200 words explaining how important the factors you choose are for job satisfaction. Provide reasons and examples to support your opinions.

TOPIC 9

Most people experience difficult periods during their lives. At such times, they need the support of family and friends.

Explain how family members and friends can support a person who is having temporary difficulty of some sort. Write a composition of about 200 words to explain your opinion on this subject. Be specific and provide examples and reasons to support your opinion.

TOPIC 10

Volunteers make it possible for small service agencies to reach people who need assistance of some kind. However, some people argue that volunteers who are not professionally trained are usually more of a liability than a benefit to service agencies.

Explain your opinion about the value of volunteers in service agencies. Write a composition of about 200 words in which you provide reasons and examples to support your opinion.

TOPIC 11

Some people feel that many essential goods and services should be paid for by the government through taxes: electricity, water, natural gas, medicine, and others. Other people think consumers should continue to pay for the goods and services they use.

What is your opinion about the way essential goods and services should be paid for—by the government or at cost to individuals? Write a composition of about 200 words in which you explain your answer to this question. Provide reasons and examples to support your opinion.

TOPIC 12

Some people think handguns should be banned because they are used to commit many violent crimes. Others say that the constitutionally granted right to bear arms, including handguns, is an important one to protect in this day and age.

Do you think handguns should be banned or not? Write a composition of about 200 words in which you explain your opinion on this question. Provide reasons and examples to support your opinion.

TOPIC 13

Many employers now offer alternatives to the traditional workweek schedule. Some of those alternatives are working part time, working flexible hours, and working at home without a fixed schedule.

What kind of workweek schedule would you choose for yourself, if you could? Write a composition of about 200 words explaining why you would like the workweek schedule you would choose. Provide reasons and examples to support your explanation.

TOPIC 14

Credit cards have changed Americans' spending habits. The use of credit cards has benefited some Americans and caused problems for others.

Explain how using credit cards can be beneficial or problematic, or both. Write a composition of about 200 words to present your views. Provide reasons and examples to support your opinions.

TOPIC 15

At some point in your life, you became aware that you no longer thought and acted as a child does but that you had entered a more mature stage of your life.

How did you come to know that you had become an adult? Write a composition of about 200 words explaining your answer to this question. Give specific examples that demonstrate your points.

The Writing Process: A Summary

This lesson reviews what you should do at each stage in the writing process. It also offers some suggestions and comments that are not offered in Chapter 2. When you are writing an essay, you may wish to use parts of this lesson as a guide to remind yourself of the things you should do during each stage of the writing process.

Budget Your Time

As you practice writing essays, you will probably find that it is not difficult to complete an essay in 45 minutes. You need to be careful, however, not to use up so much time in the first two stages of the process that you have too little time for the last two stages. The chart that follows suggests a way to budget 45 minutes for writing an essay. Try following this schedule to see how well it works for you.

Stage of the Writing Process	Minutes
Generating ideas	5
Organizing ideas	10
Writing	20
Revising	5
Editing	5
Total	**45**

Remember that at any point in the writing process you can make changes, add new ideas, and leave ideas out. Therefore, even if you don't feel satisfied with your cluster at the end of about 5 minutes (generating ideas), go on to the next stage. Don't let time run away while you stare at an incomplete cluster. More ideas will come to you. You may get a new idea while you are writing; if you do, you can add it to your map and return to writing.

Stages of the Writing Process

The writing process begins once you have decided on a point of view for your essay. To do that, the first steps are as follows:

- Read and reread the topic assignment to understand all of its implications.
- Underline important words.

Then you put your point of view into words:

- Write a question using some of the words you underlined in the topic.
- Write an answer to the question.

The answer you write is the point of view or central idea your essay will be about.

The following is a summary of the things you should do at each stage of the writing process.

Generating Ideas. With your point of view in mind, make notes about the ideas that come to you. Remember that you are writing to explain your thoughts to someone else. Pretend that you are thinking of things to tell a friend about your point of view.

- Write a brief version of your point of view

    at the top of a sheet of paper, if you brainstorm.

    in a circle in the middle of a sheet of paper, if you cluster.
- Make notes in words or short phrases, not in sentences, about every idea that crosses your mind, even if it seems ridiculous.

    Write your notes

    in a list, if your brainstorm.

    inside circles on extensions from the point-of-view circle, if you cluster.

Organizing Ideas. Group ideas that are related.

- Decide how to group your notes, and create labels for the groups

    By rewriting the notes in labeled lists, if you brainstorm.

    By coding circles, if you cluster.
- Make a map. Write your point of view in the middle of a piece of paper. Write the labels you created on extensions from the point of view, and copy your organized notes in groups at the ends of the extensions.

Write a Draft. Follow your map to write the draft for your essay.

- Write the introductory paragraph. Introduce the topic of the essay in the 1st sentence. State your point of view in the 2nd sentence.
- Write one paragraph for each group of supporting ideas and details from your map. Begin with a topic sentence. Write supporting sentences that develop examples, details, or reasons.
- Write a concluding or summary paragraph. Restate your point of view and summarize important ideas that are in the middle of your essay.

Revise the Draft. Look critically at the point of view, the content, the organization, and the conclusion or summary. Ask the following questions, and make changes that will improve your essay:

- Is the central idea, the point of view, clearly stated in one sentence at the beginning of the essay?

- Are there two or three paragraphs with examples and reasons that support the point of view?
- Does each supporting paragraph contain specific examples & details?
- Are there words and phrases that show how the supporting ideas relate to the central idea?
- Does the summary or conclusion pull together all the important ideas in the essay—without bringing in any new ideas?

Edit the Draft. Make sure that the essay reads smoothly. Correct any errors you find. You may be able to make improvements if you

- shorten sentences.
- combine sentences.
- add transition words.
- correct grammatical, structural, and mechanical problems.

After you have worked through all five stages of the writing process, reread your finished essay one more time as a final check. Make any improvements you still have time to make.

Some Suggestions

The following are suggestions about things you can do at the various stages of the writing process.

Generating Ideas and Organizing Ideas. After you have become comfortable with the writing process, you may be able to save time by combining steps. You may find that you can do your brainstorming in the form of a map. At the same time ideas are coming to you, you may realize how they should be grouped. If so, make mapping the first step of the writing process.

Writing. Write legibly. An illegible essay cannot be scored. Don't forget to indent paragraphs. Write on every other line so that when you revise and edit, there is room to add words, phrases, and sentences. (You will have to add changes on your draft because you will probably not have enough time to copy your essay over.)

Revising and Editing. Use the following marks when you edit so that the essay readers will understand what you intend.

Symbol	Purpose
$\wedge$	To insert a letter, a word, a phrase, or a sentence
——	To cross out words, phrases, or sentences
/	To change a capital letter to a lower case letter

Symbol	Purpose
R̂	To change a lower case letter to a capital letter
⟲	To move a word, a phrase, or a sentence
¶	To indicate a new paragraph
⌐⌐	To move a paragraph

The following shows an example of those revising and editing symbols being used.

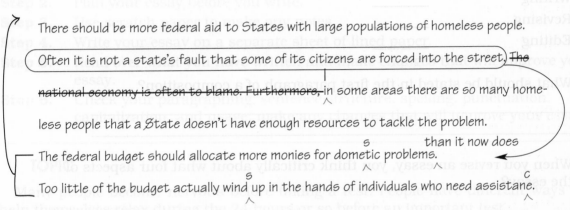

After you have written several essays, take the Practice Tests in this book. The Answers and Explanations entries for those tests will help you evaluate your essays. Finally, take the Simulated Test starting on page 75 and check your answers. Use the Performance Analysis Charts to record your scores and to find out whether you need to review before you take the GED.

Practice Test 1

Performance Analysis Chart

Directions: After you have used the guidelines in the Answers and Explanations section of this book to score your essay, make a record of your evaluation here:

Write the score of your essay in the box at the right.

List some of the strong points of your essay.

List some of the weak points of your essay.

List improvements that you plan to make when you work on your next essay.

Practice Test 2

Time: *45 minutes*
Directions: *This is a test to see how well you write. You are asked to write an essay in which you explain something or present an opinion about an issue. In preparing your essay, you should take the following steps.*

Step 1. Read the directions and the essay topic.
Step 2. Plan your essay before you write.
Step 3. Use scratch paper to make any notes.
Step 4. Write your essay on a separate sheet of lined paper.
Step 5. Read over what you have written and make changes that will improve your essay.
Step 6. Check your paragraphing, sentence structure, spelling, punctuation, capitalization, and usage; make any changes that will improve your essay.

TOPIC

Air travel has created many changes in the world. Some of these changes have improved our lives; some have made our lives more unpleasant.

How has air travel affected modern life? Write a composition of about 200 words in which you explain the positive effects, the negative effects, or both the positive and the negative effects air travel has had on our lives. Provide examples and reasons to support your opinion.

When you take the GED test, you will have 45 minutes to write about the topic you are assigned. Try to write this essay in 45 minutes. Write legibly and use a pen so that your writing will be easy to read. Any notes that you make on scratch paper will not be counted as part of your score.

After you complete this essay, you can judge its effectiveness by using the Essay Scoring Guide and Model Essays in the Answers and Explanations section of this book.

Answers are on pages 100–101.

Practice Test 2

Performance Analysis Chart

Directions: After you have used the guidelines in the Answers and Explanations section of this book to score your essay, make a record of your evaluation here:

Write the score of your essay in the box at the right.

List some of the strong points of your essay.

List some of the weak points of your essay.

List improvements that you plan to make when you work on your next essay.

Simulated Test
Part I

Time: 75 minutes

Directions: The following items are based on a paragraph that contains numbered sentences. Some of the sentences contain errors in sentence structure, usage, or mechanics. **A few sentences, however, may be correct as written**. Read the paragraph and then answer the items that follow it. For each item, choose the answer that would result in the most effective writing of the sentence or sentences. The best answer must be consistent with the meaning and tone of the rest of the paragraph.

Directions: Choose the one best answer to each item.

Items 1 to 9 refer to the following paragraph.

(1)Shopping by mail has become very popular. (2)You can look through a catalog, put in an order, and receiving your selection in the mail without having to visit a store. (3)Mail order shopping, like all types of buying, require that you use good judgment and care. (4)Many catalogs claim to offer products that are substantially below the list price, but local stores often have equally low prices. (5)If you decide to order something by mail, be sure to fill out all forms completely and clearly. (6)Problems occur if you forget to fill in an address or are unclear about wear a gift is to be sent. (7)Its very important that item numbers and quantities are clearly written. (8)Make certain that you haven't passed a cut-off date for orders, especially around holiday time. (9)The Winter coat you plan to give your grandmother on Christmas, for example, may have to be ordered by a specified date. (10)Carefully add the prices in your order, and remembering to include tax, postage, and handling in the total. (11)Either a check or a credit card payment are usually acceptable. (12)There should be a record kept by you of your order, and it should be checked right away upon delivery.

1. Sentence 2: **You can look through a catalog, put in an <u>order, and receiving your selection</u> in the mail without having to visit a store.**

Which of the following is the best way to write the underlined portion of this sentence? If you think the original is the best way, choose option (1).

(1) order, and receiving your selection
(2) order and receiving your selection
(3) order and, receiving your selection
(4) order and received your selection
(5) order, and receive your selection

2. Sentence 3: **Mail order shopping, like all types of buying, <u>require that you use</u> good judgment and care.**

Which of the following is the best way to write the underlined portion of this sentence? If you think the original is the best way, choose option (1).

(1) require that you use
(2) requires that you use
(3) required that you use
(4) require that you used
(5) require that one use

3. Sentence 4: **Many catalogs claim to offer products that are substantially below the list <u>price, but local stores</u> often have equally low prices.**

Which of the following is the best way to write the underlined portion of this sentence? If you think the original is the best way, choose option (1).

(1) price, but local stores
(2) price but, local stores
(3) price; but local stores
(4) price. But local stores
(5) price but local stores

4. Sentence 6: **Problems occur if you forget to fill in an address or are unclear about wear a gift is to be sent.**

What correction should be made to this sentence?

(1) change the spelling of <u>occur</u> to <u>ocurr</u>
(2) replace <u>you forget</u> with <u>one forgets</u>
(3) change the spelling of <u>address</u> to <u>adress</u>
(4) change <u>are</u> to <u>were</u>
(5) replace <u>wear</u> with <u>where</u>

5. Sentence 7: **Its very important that item numbers and quantities are clearly written.**

What correction should be made to this sentence?

(1) change <u>Its</u> to <u>It's</u>
(2) insert a comma after <u>numbers</u>
(3) change <u>are</u> to <u>is</u>
(4) change <u>written</u> to <u>wrote</u>
(5) no correction is necessary

6. Sentence 9: **The Winter coat you plan to give your grandmother on Christmas, for example, may have to be ordered by a specified date.**

What correction should be made to this sentence?

(1) change <u>Winter</u> to <u>winter</u>
(2) replace <u>your</u> with <u>you're</u>
(3) change <u>grandmother</u> to <u>Grandmother</u>
(4) remove the comma after <u>example</u>
(5) no correction is necessary

7. Sentence 10: **Carefully add the prices in your order, and remembering to include tax, postage, and handling in the total.**

What correction should be made to this sentence?

(1) change <u>add</u> to <u>adding</u>
(2) replace <u>your</u> with <u>one's</u>
(3) remove the comma after <u>order</u>
(4) change <u>remembering</u> to <u>remember</u>
(5) no correction is necessary

8. Sentence 11: **Either a check or a credit card payment are usually acceptable.**

What correction should be made to this sentence?

(1) insert a comma after <u>check</u>
(2) change <u>credit card</u> to <u>Credit Card</u>
(3) change <u>are</u> to <u>is</u>
(4) change the spelling of <u>usually</u> to <u>usualy</u>
(5) change the spelling of <u>acceptable</u> to <u>acceptible</u>

9. Sentence 12: **There should be a record kept by you of your order, and it should be checked right away upon delivery.**

If you rewrote sentence 12 beginning with

<u>Keep a record of your order, and check</u>

the next word should be

(1) there
(2) it
(3) your
(4) right
(5) that

GO ON TO THE NEXT PAGE

Items 10 to 19 refer to the following paragraph.

(1)Some of the job openings in your area can be found in the employment section of your daily newspaper. (2)Job hunters often check the Sunday paper seeing as it contains more job listings than weekday editions do. (3)Many advertisements advise applicants to send his resume and a cover letter to a particular person or box number. (4)Select some plain stationery if you decide to answer a "help wanted" ad. (5)After checking the spelling and title of the person which will receive your application, write a short cover letter. (6)You could begin by saying, "I am enclosing my resume in response to one's advertisement for the secretary in the July 17th issue of the Middletown Times." (7)Explain what you're doing currently if you're unemployed, describe past job or volunteer work you've done. (8)You may have special achievements. (9)If they are relevant to the position, you should emphasize them. (10)To show that you are good at initiating action, you could close by saying that you will call for an appointment. (11)Check your resume of past experience to see that you have given your present address, and telephone number. (12)Address the envelope carefully, add the correct postage, and put it in the morning mail for quickest delivery.

10. Sentence 2: **Job hunters often check the Sunday paper seeing as it contains more job listings than weekday editions do.**

    What correction should be made to this sentence?

    (1) change Sunday to sunday
    (2) insert a comma after paper
    (3) replace seeing as with because
    (4) replace it contains with they contain
    (5) replace than with then

11. Sentence 3: **Many advertisements advise applicants to send his resume and cover letter to a particular person or box number.**

    What correction should be made to this sentence?

    (1) change the spelling of advertisements to advertisements
    (2) replace his with a
    (3) insert a comma after resume
    (4) change box number to Box Number
    (5) no correction is necessary

12. Sentence 4: **Select some plain stationery if you decide to answer a "help wanted" ad.**

    If you rewrote sentence 4 beginning with

    If you decide to answer a "help wanted"

    the next word should be

    (1) ad.
    (2) ad,
    (3) ad;
    (4) one,
    (5) one

13. Sentence 5: **After checking the spelling and title of the person which will receive your application, write a short cover letter.**

    Which of the following is the best way to write the underlined portion of this sentence? If you think the original is the best way, choose option (1).

    (1) person which will receive
    (2) person, which will receive
    (3) person who will receive
    (4) person, who will receive
    (5) person which received

14. Sentence 6: **You could begin by saying, "I am enclosing my resume in response to one's advertisement for a secretary in the July 17th issue of the Middletown Times."**

    What correction should be made to this sentence?

    (1) insert a comma after resume
    (2) replace one's with your
    (3) change the spelling of secretary to secratery
    (4) change July to july
    (5) change Times to times

15. Sentence 7: **Explain what you're doing currently if you're unemployed, describe past jobs or volunteer work you've done.**

    What correction should be made to this sentence?

    (1) replace currently if with currently. If
    (2) replace past with passed
    (3) replace you've with you'ave
    (4) change done to did
    (5) no correction is necessary

16. Sentences 8 and 9: **You may have special achievements. If they are relevant to the position, you should emphasize them.**

    The most effective combination of sentences 8 and 9 would include which of the following groups of words?

    (1) if you have any which are
    (2) and if they are relevant
    (3) achievements that are special
    (4) achievements that are relevant
    (5) you should emphasize that

17. Sentence 10: **To show that you are good at initiating action, you could close by saying that you will call for an appointment.**

    What correction should be made to this sentence?

    (1) change are to were
    (2) change the spelling of initiating to iniciating
    (3) remove the comma after action
    (4) replace you could with to
    (5) no correction is necessary.

18. Sentence 11: **Check your resume of past experience to see <u>that you have given your present address, and</u> telephone number.**

    Which of the following is the best way to write the underlined portion of this sentence? If you think the original is the best way, choose option (1).

    (1) that you have given your present address, and
    (2) that you have given your present address and
    (3) that you give your present address, and
    (4) that you have given your present address and
    (5) that you have given your present address, and

19. Sentence 12: **Address the envelope carefully, add the correct postage, and put it in the morning mail for quickest delivery.**

    What correction should be made to this sentence?

    (1) replace carefully with careful
    (2) remove the comma after postage
    (3) replace it with your application
    (4) replace mail with male
    (5) replace quickest with most quick

GO ON TO THE NEXT PAGE

Items 20 to 28 refer to the following paragraph.

(1)Computers have many roles in the world of music, they have been used to compose music since the 1950s. (2)In 1956 a man named LeJaren Hiller composed the first piece of computer music at the university of Illinois. (3)John Cage is another name associated with early computer music. (4)Included among the first computer musicians was a group at Bell Telephone Laboratories that recorded the album, Music from Mathematics. (5)That title, incidentally, describes computer music in general; notes and rythms are selected by mathematical rules. (6)Because the computer makes many of these selections some people claim that computer musicians are not truly creative. (7)On the other hand, there are those who felt that it requires an exceptional imagination to write good computer music. (8)Computers is used more often to produce sounds than to compose music. (9)By pressing a few keys on special computers, strange and sometimes beautiful sounds can be made by anyone. (10)Sometimes pieces of old music have missing portions. (11)Computers have been used to write music that is consistent with the remaining pieces. (12)In addition, computers are improving the efficiency with which music is printed and stored.

20. Sentence 1: **Computers have many roles in the world of music, they have been used to compose music since the 1950s.**

What correction should be made to this sentence?

   (1) replace <u>Computers have</u> with <u>The computer has</u>
   (2) change the spelling of <u>roles</u> to <u>rolls</u>
   (3) replace <u>music, they</u> with <u>music. They</u>
   (4) change <u>have been</u> to <u>has been</u>
   (5) insert a comma after <u>used</u>

21. Sentence 2: **In 1956 a man named LeJaren Hiller composed the first piece of computer music at the university of Illinois.**

What correction should be made to this sentence?

   (1) insert a comma after <u>Hiller</u>
   (2) change <u>composed</u> to <u>composes</u>
   (3) replace <u>pieced</u> with <u>peace</u>
   (4) change <u>university</u> to <u>University</u>
   (5) change <u>Illinois</u> to <u>illinois</u>

22. Sentence 4: **Included among the first computer musicians was a group at Bell Telephone Laboratories that recorded the album, <u>Music from Mathematics</u>.**

What correction should be made to this sentence?

   (1) change <u>was</u> to <u>were</u>
   (2) change <u>Laboratories</u> to <u>laboratories</u>
   (3) remove the comma after <u>album</u>
   (4) change the spelling of <u>Mathematics</u> to <u>Mathmatics</u>
   (5) no correction is necessary

23. Sentence 5: **That title, incidentally, describes computer music in general; notes and rythms are selected by mathematical rules.**

What correction should be made to this sentence?

   (1) remove the comma after <u>title</u>
   (2) change the spelling of <u>incidentally</u> to <u>incedentally</u>
   (3) change <u>describes</u> to <u>describing</u>
   (4) replace <u>general; notes</u> with <u>general, notes</u>
   (5) change the spelling of <u>rythms</u> to <u>rhythms</u>

GO ON TO THE NEXT PAGE

24. Sentence 6: **Because the computer makes many of these selections some people claim that computer musicians are not truly creative.**

What correction should be made to this sentence?

(1) change <u>makes</u> to <u>made</u>
(2) change <u>makes</u> to <u>make</u>
(3) change the spelling of <u>truly</u> to <u>truely</u>
(4) insert a comma after <u>selections</u>
(5) insert a comma after <u>claim</u>

25. Sentence 7: **On the other <u>hand, there are those who felt</u> that it requires an exceptional imagination to write good computer music.**

Which of the following is the best way to write the underlined portion of this sentence? If you think the original is the best way, choose option (1).

(1) hand, there are those who felt
(2) hand there are those who felt
(3) hand, there is those who felt
(4) hand, there are those which felt
(5) hand, there are those who feel

26. Sentence 8: **Computers <u>is used more often to produce sounds than</u> to compose music.**

Which of the following is the best way to write the underlined portion of this sentence? If you think the original is the best way, choose option (1).

(1) is used more often to produce sounds than
(2) are used more often to produce sounds than
(3) is used more to produce sounds often than
(4) is used more often to produce sounds, then
(5) is used more often to produce sounds as

27. Sentence 9: **By pressing a few keys on special computers, <u>strange and sometimes beautiful sounds can be made by anyone</u>.**

Which of the following is the best way to write the underlined portion of this sentence? If you think the original is the best way, choose option (1).

(1) strange and sometimes beautiful sounds can be made by anyone.
(2) strange, and sometimes beautiful sounds can be made by anyone.
(3) strange and sometimes beautiful sounds can be made, by anyone.
(4) anyone can make strange and sometimes beautiful sounds.
(5) anyone made strange and sometimes beautiful sounds.

28. Sentences 11 and 12: **Computers have been used to write music that is consistent with the remaining pieces. In addition, computers are improving the efficiency with which music is printed and stored.**

The most effective combination of sentences 11 and 12 would include which of the following groups of words?

(1) pieces, and are an improvement
(2) pieces, and are also improving
(3) pieces and also to improve
(4) pieces; and also they are
(5) pieces so that they can

(1)Almost everyone has experienced insomnia a problem in getting to sleep or staying asleep. (2)In California there was now a special place for studying the problem: the Stanford University Sleep Disorders Clinic. (3)At the clinic, researchers have found that serious difficulties in sleeping may be due to problems that require medical attention, such as heart, lung, or kidney disease. (4)When most people can't fall asleep or wake up too early, however, some simple remedies are often effective. (5)Drinking a cup of warm milk or eating an apple may help; both contain a natural relaxant. (6)A cup of coffee, a glass of cola, or a mug of cocoa may be a bedtime favorite of your's, but you should avoid all three. (7)If you take medicine for a cold, a weight problem, or depression, asking your doctor whether it could cause sleeplessness. (8)During the daytime try to work out the things that are bothering you then maybe you won't worry about them at night. (9)Think twice before taking alcohol or a sleep medication, and don't ever take them together. (10)You can become dependent on both, and taken together they can kill one. (11)When you can't sleep, it is probably better to turn on a light and do something than lying in the dark worrying about it.

29. Sentence 1: **Almost everyone <u>has experienced insomnia a problem</u> in getting to sleep or staying asleep.**

Which of the following is the best way to write the underlined portion of this sentence? If you think the original is the best way, choose option (1).

(1) has experienced insomnia a problem
(2) have experienced insomnia
a problem
(3) having experienced insomnia
a problem
(4) experienced insomnia a problem
(5) has experienced insomnia, a problem

30. Sentence 2: **In California there was now a special place for studying the problem: the Stanford University Sleep Disorders Clinic.**

What correction should be made to this sentence?

(1) replace <u>there</u> with <u>their</u>
(2) change <u>was</u> to <u>is</u>
(3) change the spelling of <u>studying</u> to <u>studing</u>
(4) change <u>Clinic</u> to <u>clinic</u>
(5) no correction is necessary

31. Sentence 3: **At the clinic, researchers have found that serious difficulties in sleeping may be due to problems that require medical attention, such as heart, lung, or kidney disease.**

What correction should be made to this sentence?

(1) change <u>clinic</u> to <u>Clinic</u>
(2) change <u>researchers</u> to <u>Researchers</u>
(3) replace <u>due</u> with <u>do</u>
(4) remove the comma after <u>lung</u>
(5) no correction is necessary

32. Sentence 4: **When most people can't fall asleep or wake up too early, however, some simple remedies are often effective.**

If you rewrote sentence 4 beginning with

<u>For most people with problems falling asleep or</u>

the next word should be

(1) have
(2) having
(3) woken
(4) waking
(5) wokening

GO ON TO THE NEXT PAGE

33. Sentence 6: **A cup of coffee, a glass of cola, or a mug of cocoa may be a bedtime favorite of your's, but you should avoid all three.**

What correction should be made to this sentence?

(1) change the spelling of <u>coffee</u> to <u>cofee</u>

(2) remove <u>a mug of</u>

(3) change the spelling of <u>your's</u> to <u>yours</u>

(4) remove the comma after <u>but</u>

(5) replace <u>all three</u> with <u>it</u>

34. Sentence 7: **If you take medicine for a cold, a weight problem, or <u>depression, asking your doctor whether it</u> could cause sleeplessness.**

Which of the following is the best way to write the underlined portion of this sentence? If you think the original is the best way, choose option (1).

(1) depression, asking your doctor whether it

(2) depression ask your doctor whether it

(3) depression, ask your doctor whether it

(4) depression, asking one's doctor whether it

(5) depression, asking your doctor whether they

35. Sentence 8: **During the daytime try to work out the things that are bothering <u>you then maybe you won't worry</u> about them at night.**

Which of the following is the best way to write the underlined portion of this sentence? If you think the original is the best way, choose option (1).

(1) you then maybe you won't worry

(2) one then maybe you won't worry

(3) you, maybe you won't worry

(4) you then, maybe you won't worry

(5) you, and maybe you won't worry

36. Sentence 10: **You can become dependent on both, and <u>taken together, they can kill one</u>.**

Which of the following is the best way to write the underlined portion of this sentence? If you think the original is the best way, choose option (1).

(1) taken together, they can kill one.

(2) took together, they can kill one.

(3) taken together they can kill one.

(4) taken together, you can die.

(5) taken together, they can kill you.

37. Sentence 11: **When you can't sleep, it is probably better to turn on a light and do something than lying in the dark worrying about it.**

What correction should be made to this sentence?

(1) replace <u>can't</u> with <u>can'nt</u>

(2) replace <u>better</u> with <u>more good</u>

(3) replace <u>to turn</u> with <u>turning</u>

(4) replace <u>than</u> with <u>as</u>

(5) replace <u>lying</u> with <u>to lie</u>

Items 38 to 47 refer to the following paragraph.

(1)When people take on a second job, they often work at night, thus, such work has come to be known as "moonlighting." (2) Moonlighters decide to work another job in addition to their full-time employment for a variety of reasons. (3)One of the main reasons is extra money. (4)It is convenient to have extra money on hand as Holidays such as Christmas and Hanukkah approach. (5)Another common reason people moonlight being pleasure. (6)A singer which works in a factory all week, for example, might enjoy singing at weekend birthday parties and weddings. (7)There may be a case of someone wanting to moonlight, but he needs to find out how his present employer feels about second jobs, first. (8)In contracts there is sometimes a line stating how that the employee will work only one job. (9)There are usually one of two reasons behind this line. (10)The employer may be concerned about the employee's doing extra work. (11)The employer may worry that the employee will be too tired to function efficiently on his full-time job. (12)The employer may also want to protect against an employee's using knowledge gained at his regular job to help a competitor. (13)After making sure that there is'nt such a statement in his contract, the employee is free to join the growing ranks of moonlighters.

38. Sentence 1: **When people take on a second job, they often work at night, thus, such work has come to be known as "moonlighting."**

    Which of the following is the best way to write the underlined portion of this sentence? If you think the original is the best way, choose option (1).

    (1) they often work at night, thus,
    (2) he often works at night, thus,
    (3) they often works at night, thus,
    (4) they often worked at night, thus,
    (5) they often work at night; thus,

39. Sentence 3: **One of the main reasons is extra money.**

    Which of the following is the best way to write the underlined portion of this sentence? If you think the original is the best way, choose option (1).

    (1) One of the main reasons is
    (2) One of the main reasons, is
    (3) One of the main reasons was
    (4) One of the main reasons being
    (5) One of the main reasons were

40. Sentence 4: **It is convenient to have extra money on hand as Holidays such as Christmas and Hanukkah approach.**

    What correction should be made to this sentence?

    (1) change is to being
    (2) change the spelling of convenient to conveniant
    (3) change Holidays to holidays
    (4) change Christmas to christmas
    (5) no correction is necessary

41. Sentence 5: **Another common reason people moonlight being pleasure.**

    What correction should be made to this sentence?

    (1) change moonlight to moonlights
    (2) insert a comma after moonlight
    (3) change being to is
    (4) change being to was
    (5) change the spelling of pleasure to plesure

42. Sentence 6: **A singer which works in a factory all week, for example, might enjoy singing at weekend birthday parties and weddings.**

What correction should be made to this sentence?

(1) replace <u>which</u> with <u>who</u>
(2) replace <u>week</u> with <u>weak</u>
(3) remove the comma after <u>example</u>
(4) change <u>weekend</u> to <u>Weekend</u>
(5) change <u>birthday</u> to <u>Birthday</u>

43. Sentence 7: **There may be a case of someone wanting to moonlight, but he needs to find out how his present employer feels about second jobs, first.**

If you rewrote sentence 7 beginning with

<u>When someone</u>

the next word should be

(1) wanting
(2) wants
(3) who
(4) needing
(5) feeling

44. Sentence 8: **In contracts there <u>is sometimes a line stating how that the</u> employee will work only one job.**

Which of the following is the best way to write the underlined portion of this sentence? If you think the original is the best way, choose option (1).

(1) is sometimes a line stating how that the
(2) are sometimes a line stating how the
(3) is sometimes a line, stating that the
(4) is sometimes a line stated how that the
(5) is sometimes a line stating that the

45. Sentence 9: <u>**There are usually one of two**</u> **reasons behind this line.**

Which of the following is the best way to write the underlined portion of this sentence? If you think the original is the best way, choose option (1).

(1) There are usually one of two
(2) There is usually one of two
(3) Usually there are one of two
(4) Usually there were one of two
(5) Usually there being one of two

46. Sentence 10 and 11: **The employer may be concerned about the employee's doing extra work. The employer may worry that the employee will be too tired to function efficiently on his full-time job.**

The most effective combination of sentences 10 and 11 would include which of the following groups of words?

(1) The employer may be too tired
(2) work, and the employer may worry
(3) that he will be functioning extra
(4) too concerned and tired to function
(5) being too tired to

47. Sentence 13: **After making sure that there is'nt such a statement in his contract, the employee is free to join the growing ranks of moonlighters.**

What correction should be made to this sentence?

(1) replace <u>there</u> with <u>they're</u>
(2) replace <u>is'nt</u> with <u>isn't</u>
(3) replace <u>that</u> with <u>if</u>
(4) remove the comma after <u>contract</u>
(5) no correction is necessary

Items 48 to 55 refer to the following paragraph.

(1)Football, like many other sports, having changed a lot over the years. (2)The rules bears only a passing resemblance to those of the original games. (3)The earliest form of football was probably played in England during the 11th century. (4)For many years, football, like today's game of soccer, were solely a kicking game. (5)Then in 1823 an English player named William Webb Ellis grew so frustrated by his mistakes that he carried the ball. (6)After officials had taken time to think about what they see, they decided to allow carrying in a new sport, football. (7)The first college game was held between Rutgers and Princeton in new Jersey on November 6, 1869. (8)Princeton won that first game, and fierce competition between the two teams continues to this day. (9)If you are interested in seeing historic records of past games important players, and famous coaches, you might want to visit New Jersey. (10)You will find the headquarters of the National Football Foundation and Hall of Fame if you go to New Brunswick.

48. Sentence 1: **Football, like many other sports, having changed a lot over the years.**

    Which of the following is the best way to write the underlined portion of this sentence? If you think the original is the best way, choose option (1).

    (1) sports, having changed a lot
    (2) sports having changed a lot
    (3) sports, have changed a lot
    (4) sports, has changed a lot
    (5) sports, has changed, a lot

49. Sentence 2: **The rules bears only a passing resemblance to those of the original games.**

    What correction should be made to this sentence?

    (1) change bears to bear
    (2) change the spelling of resemblance to resemblence
    (3) insert a comma after resemblance
    (4) replace those with that
    (5) no correction is necessary

50. Sentence 4: **For many years, football, like today's game of soccer, were solely a kicking game.**

    Which of the following is the best way to write the underlined portion of this sentence? If you think the original is the best way, choose option (1).

    (1) like today's game of soccer, were
    (2) like today's game of soccer were
    (3) like today's game of soccer, was
    (4) like today's game of soccer, being
    (5) like today's game of soccer, been

51. Sentence 5: **Then in 1823 an English player named William Webb Ellis grew so frustrated by his mistakes that he carried the ball.**

    What correction should be made to this sentence?

    (1) change English to english
    (2) change grew to grows
    (3) replace his with his'
    (4) replace that with as
    (5) no correction is necessary

52. Sentence 6: **After officials <u>had taken time to think about what they see</u>, they decided to allow carrying in a new sport, football.**

Which of the following is the best way to write the underlined portion of this sentence? If you think the original is the best way, choose option (1).

(1) had taken time to think about what they see,
(2) taken time to think about what they see,
(3) had taken time to think about what they have seen,
(4) had taken time to think about what they saw,
(5) had taken time to think about what they saw

53. Sentence 7: **The first college game was held between Rutgers and Princeton in new Jersey on November 6, 1869.**

What correction should be made to this sentence?

(1) change <u>college</u> to <u>College</u>
(2) change <u>was</u> to <u>is</u>
(3) insert a comma after <u>Rutgers</u>
(4) change <u>new</u> to <u>New</u>
(5) change <u>Jersey</u> to <u>jersey</u>

54. Sentence 9: **If you are interested in seeing historic records of past games important players, and famous coaches, you might want to visit New Jersey.**

What correction should be made to this sentence?

(1) change <u>are</u> to <u>is</u>
(2) replace <u>past</u> with <u>passed</u>
(3) insert a comma after <u>games</u>
(4) remove the comma after <u>players</u>
(5) replace <u>you might</u> with <u>one might</u>

55. Sentence 10: **You will find the headquarters of the National Football Foundation and Hall of Fame if you go to New Brunswick**

If you rewrote sentence 10 beginning with

<u>in New Brunswick.</u>

the next word should be

(1) if you go
(2) the Hall of Fame
(3) headquarters of the
(4) finding the headquarter
(5) you will find

Check your answers. Correct answers begin on page 102.

Simulated Test
Part II

Time: 45 minutes

Directions: This is a test to see how well you write. You are asked to write an essay in which you explain something or present an option about an issue. In preparing your essay, you should take the following steps:

1. Read carefully the directions and the essay topic given below.

2. Plan your essay carefully before you write.

3. Use scratch paper to make any notes.

4. Write your essay on a separate sheet of lined paper.

5. Read carefully what you have written and make any changes that will improve your essay.

6. Check your paragraphs, sentence structure, spelling, punctuation, capitalization, and usage, and make any necessary corrections.

Directions: When you take the GED test, you will have 45 minutes to write about the topic you are assigned. Try to write this essay in 45 minutes. Write legibly and use a pen so that your writing will be easy to read. Any notes that you make on scratch paper will not be counted as part of your score.

After you complete this essay, you can judge its effectiveness by using the Essay Scoring Guide and Model Essays in the Answers and Explanations section of this book.

TOPIC

Restrictions on smoking in public areas vary from place to place in the United States. Many people think smoking in public areas should be strictly regulated; others disagree.

Do you think there should be restrictions on smoking in public places? Write a composition of about 200 words in which you explain your answer to this question. Provide examples and reasons to support your opinion.

Answers begin on page 105.

SIMULATED TEST

Performance Analysis Chart
Part I

Directions: Circle the number of each item that you got correct on the Simulated Test. Count how many items you got correct in each row; count how many items you got correct in each column. Write the amount correct per row and column as the numerator in the fraction in the appropriate "Total Correct" box. (The denominators represent the total number of items in the row or column.) Write the grand total correct over the denominator **55** at the lower right corner of the chart. (For example, if you got *50* items correct, write *50* so that the fraction reads 50/**55**.)

Item Type	Usage (Unit 1)	Sentence Structure (Unit 2)	Mechanics (Unit 3)	TOTAL CORRECT
Construction Shift	9, 43	16, 28, 32, 46, 55	12	/8
Sentence Correction	8, 11, 14, 19, 22, 30, 42, 49	7, 10, 15, 20, 37, 41, 51	4, 5, 6, 17, 21, 23, 24, 31, 33, 40, 47, 53, 54	/28
Sentence Revision	2, 13, 25, 26, 36, 39, 45, 50, 52	1, 27, 34, 35, 38, 44, 48	3, 18, 29	/19
TOTAL CORRECT	/19	/19	/17	/55

The (Unit 1) chapters named in parentheses indicate where in the Writing Skills instruction of the *New Revised Cambridge GED Program: Comprehensive Book* and the *New Revised Cambridge GED Program: Writing Skills* you can find specific instruction about the areas of grammar you encountered on the Simulated Test.

On the chart, items are classified as Construction Shift, Sentence Correction, and Sentence Revision. These three item types are introduced in Unit 1, Chapter 4, Lesson 1 in the *New Revised Cambridge GED Program: Comprehensive Book* and in the *New Revised Cambridge GED Program: Writing Skills*.

Part II

Directions: After you have used the guidelines in the Answers and Explanations section of this book to score your essay, make a record of your evaluation here:

Write the score of your essay in the box at the right.

List some of the strong points of your essay.

List some of the weak points of your essay.

List improvements that you plan to make when you work on your next essay.

Answers & Explanations

Chapter 2

The Writing Process

Lesson 2 Understanding Essay Topics

1. **The first part** of the topic contains the background.

2. The subject of the composition should be **required school attendance.**

3. This should be written about the subject: **a 200-word composition that explains whether I think school should be required for young people until they are in their late teens.**

4. **(a)** You might have underlined *American youth, required, school, law, stay in school, 16 years old, late teens.*

   (b) A sample question: **Should American youths be required to stay in school until they are in their late teens?**

   (c) Three sample answers: **American youths should be required to stay in school until they are in their late teens.**
   American youths should not be required to stay in school until they are in their late teens.
   Some American youths should be required to stay in school until they are in their late teens.

Lesson 3

Topic 3
(a) **Key words:** adults, exercise regularly, vigorously, improve health, prolong lives, exercising too much, harmful, value of regular, vigorous exercise, beneficial, harmful.

(b) **Question:** Do you think regular, vigorous exercise is beneficial or harmful?

(c) **Point of View:** Regular, vigorous exercise is beneficial. Or, Regular, vigorous exercise is harmful.

(d) **Brainstorming:** Benefits: improved circulation, lowers blood pressure, tones muscles, helps to lose and/or maintain ideal weight, lowers blood cholesterol level; protects against heart disease, slows down aging process, gives more energy, more self-confidence, reduces stress and tension, builds positive self-image. Harms: accidents that injure muscles, bones, and tendons; develop knee problems and tendonitis; stresses heart problems and tendonitis.

Topic 4
(a) **Key Words:** casual, unprotected sex, dangerous, AIDS, deadly disease, spreading, adults, protect, spread of AIDS.

(b) **Question:** What can adults do to protect themselves from the spread of AIDS?

(c) **Point of View:** Adults can protect themselves from the spread of AIDS in many ways.

(d) **Brainstorming:** practice celibacy or monogamy, use condoms, get to know partner well before having sexual relations, get an HIV blood test, donate own blood, do not share needles, clean needles in bleach solution.

Lesson 4

Topic 5
(a) **Key Words:** success, wealth, material possessions, influence, power, relationships, measures success.

(b) **Question:** How do I measure success?

(c) **Point of View:** I measure success in several ways.

Topic 6
(a) **Key Words:** sports, individualized sports, team sports, choice of participating in, choose.

(b) **Question:** Would you prefer to participate in an individual or team sport?

(c) **Point of View:** I prefer participating in individual sports. Or, I prefer participating in team sports.

Cluster Maps for Topic 5, Page 30

(d) Cluster of Measures of Success

(e) Organizing Cluster

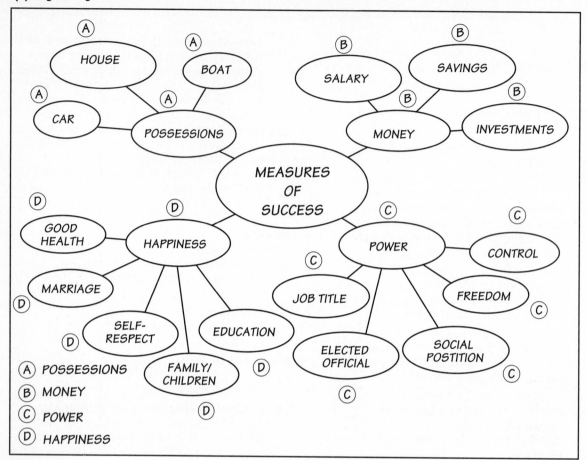

Ⓐ POSSESSIONS
Ⓑ MONEY
Ⓒ POWER
Ⓓ HAPPINESS

(f) Mapping

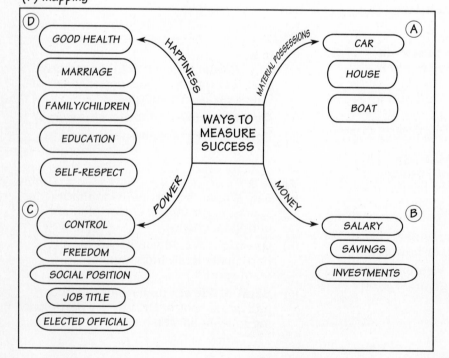

Possessions

(f) Cluster of Individual Sports

(e) Organizing Cluster

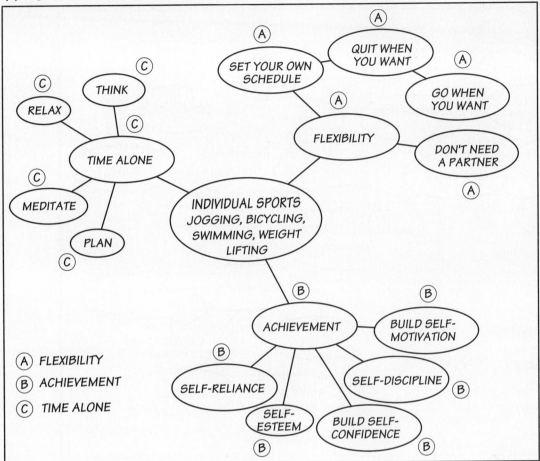

(f) Mapping

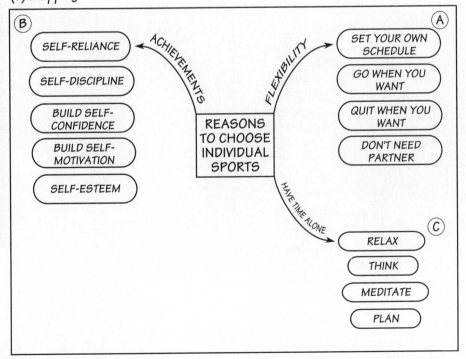

Cluster Maps for Topic 6, Page 31

(d) Cluster of Team Sports

(e) Organizing Cluster

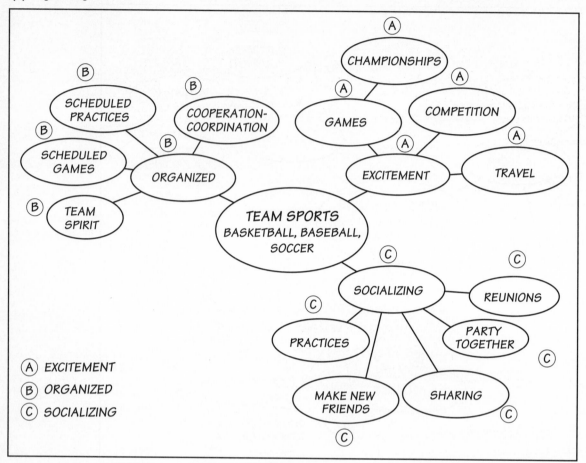

Ⓐ EXCITEMENT
Ⓑ ORGANIZED
Ⓒ SOCIALIZING

(f) Mapping

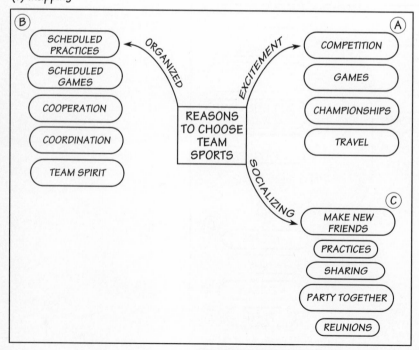

Chapter 3

Reviewing the Writing Process

Lesson 2 The Writing Process: A Summary

1. Generating Ideas **5** minutes
   Organizing Ideas **10** minutes
   Writing **20** minutes
   Revising **5** minutes
   Editing **5** minutes

2. **The point of view** should be stated in the first paragraph of a composition.

3. (a) **the point of view**
   (b) **the content**
   (c) **the organization**
   (d) **the conclusion or summary**

4. Credit Cards have enabled people (with *many* inserted, *C* capitalization marks) much earlier to posess good (with *s* insertion marks) than could have if they had to pay (with *they*, *had* insertions) ~~a lot of~~ Cash.

Essay Scoring Guide

Directions: Use the following *GED Essay Scoring Guide* and *How to Score Your Essay* as guidelines for evaluating the essays you write for the Practice Tests and the Simulated Test.

The following GED Essay Scoring Guide provides a general description of the characteristics found in GED essays that are scored by the Holistic Method.

Upper-half papers make clear a definite purpose, pursued with varying degrees of effectiveness. They also have a structure that shows evidence of some deliberate planning. The writer's control of English usage ranges from fairly reliable at 4 to confident and accomplished at 6.

6 Papers scored as a 6 tend to offer sophisticated ideas within an organizational framework that is clear and appropriate for the topic. The supporting statements are particularly effective because of their substance, specificity, or illustrative quality. The writing is vivid and precise, though it may contain an occasional flaw.

5 Papers scored as a 5 are clearly organized with effective support for each of the writer's major points. The writing offers substantive ideas, though the paper may lack the flair or grace of a 6 paper. The surface features are consistently under control, despite an occasional lapse in usage.

4 Papers scored as a 4 show evidence of the writer's organizational plan. Support, though sufficient, tends to be less extensive or convincing than that found in papers scored as a 5 or 6. The writer generally observes the conventions of accepted English usage. Some errors are usually present, but they are not severe enough to interfere significantly with the writer's main purpose.

Lower-half papers either fail to convey a purpose sufficiently or lack one entirely. Consequently, their structure ranges from rudimentary at 3, to random at 2, to absent at 1. Control of the conventions of English usage tends to follow this same gradient.

3 Papers scored as a 3 usually show some evidence of planning or development. However, the organization is often limited to a simple listing or haphazard recitation of ideas about the topic, leaving an impression of insufficiency. The 3 papers often demonstrate repeated weaknesses in accepted English usage and are generally ineffective in accomplishing the writer's purpose.

2 Papers scored as a 2 are characterized by a marked lack of development or inadequate support for ideas. The level of thought apparent in the writing is frequently unsophisticated or superficial, often marked by a listing of unsupported generalizations. Instead of suggesting a clear purpose, these papers often present conflicting purposes. Errors in accepted English usage may seriously interfere with the overall effectiveness of these papers.

1 Papers scored as a 1 leave the impression that the writer has not only *not* accomplished a purpose, but has not made any purpose apparent. The dominant feature of these papers is the lack of control. The writer stumbles both in conveying a clear plan for the paper and in expressing ideas according to the conventions of accepted English usage.

0 The zero score is reserved for papers which are blank, illegible, or written on a topic other than the one assigned.

Copyright 1985, GED Testing Service, September, 1985

Source: *The 1988 Test of General Educational Development: A Preview*, American Council on Education, 1985. Used with permission.

HOW TO SCORE YOUR ESSAY

To score your essay, compare it with the following model essays. These model essays received scores of 3 and 5, respectively.

Compare your essay with the 3 model essay. If it is as good as the 3 model essay, then assign your essay a score of 3. If it is not as good as the 3 model essay, then refer back to the answer key of the Writing Skills Predictor Test and use the descriptions of the 1 and 2 model essays to evaluate your essay. It should be easy to assign a score to your essay if you compare your essay with these model essays and their character trait analyses.

If your essay is better than the 3 model essay, compare it to the model essay that received a 5. If it is better than the 3 but not as good as the 5, then score your essay a 4. If your essay is better than the 5 model essay, then score your essay a 6.

In addition, look at the notes and character trait analyses that accompany the model essays. These comments explain the strengths and weaknesses of these essays.

Practice Test 1

Directions: Refer to the GED Essay Scoring Guide (page 96) and the model essays that follow for help in evaluating your essay.

Model Essay—Holistic Score 3

The point of view is not clearly stated.

A haphazard listing of ideas about the topic makes up the rest of the essay.

It is very very important to relax before you take a test. If not, you could really blow the test. Being uptight before a test makes you forget alot of what you already knew. You make problems for yourself. That you don't really have to. Its not easy, relaxing. Not if your nervous and scared. But it's still very important. I'm not very good at it myself. The night before a test, I get very very nervous. But I know its important to relax and I try to work at it. Sometimes I go out to a movie or something like that. Other times I stay home and try to study. I do different things to try to relax. Some work better than others.

I think the worst thing you can do the night before a test is study too much. That just makes things worse. You start thinking, boy am I dumb. I don't know anything. Which isn't true. If you've been studying. But if you go out and party too late, you won't be relaxed. You'll just be tired. The best thing is to have fun. But not too much fun. Just watch TV or talk to a friend. Then the day of the test, try and build your confidence up. Tell yourself it's going to be alright. With a good attitude, you'll probably do better on the test.

Character Trait Analysis

Point of View: The central idea is stated in the first sentence of the essay, but not clearly. The essay should be about what *the writer* does to relax before a test. The first sentence does not make that clear.

Content: The following sentences are the only ones that list activities the writer uses to relax before a test: *Sometimes I go out to a movie or something like that. Other times I stay home and try to study. I do different things to try to relax. Some work better than others.* These sentences do not report what the writer has found to be successful ways to relax or why one way works better than another. It merely lists various of the writer's activities before tests.

Organization: This essay is poorly organized. If the key idea had been stated more clearly, the writer might have been able to paragraph better and focus the ideas more sharply. There are really two ideas in the first paragraph: (1) the effects of not relaxing before a test and (2) the writer's own difficulty with relaxing. If the writer had identified those two ideas, each could have been supported with specific examples in separate paragraphs.

Conclusion or Summary: The essay lacks a restatement of the point of view and a conclusion. Rather, it ends with advice to the reader, which is not what the essay is about or what the topic assignment calls for.

Mechanics: The essay contains many sentences fragments and other mechanical errors that contribute to its limited effectiveness.

Model Essay—Holistic Score 5

States point of view and introduces middle paragraphs.

Gives examples of preparing mentally; uses specific details.

Gives examples of preparing physically; uses specific details.

Concludes, but mentions other people.

Taking tests makes many people nervous. There are several things I do to reduce my anxiety before a major test. When I can control my nervousness my score often benefits. Some activities help me to prepare mentally, and others help me to relax physically.

For me, getting ready mentally starts the day before the test. I usually do a short general review, but I try to keep from "cramming." Instead, I remind myself of all the work that I have done in the preceding weeks. I select my clothes for the next day and collect any pencils, pens, and other items I will need. Then I tell myself a few times that I know the material and am ready to do my best.

On the evening before the test, I do what I can to get rid of any physical tension I have. I start with some light exercise, followed by a hot shower or bath. Then I turn on some soft music, set my alarm, and get to bed early.

In conclusion, feeling confident and rested allows me to face an exam much more calmly. Different people take different steps to achieve this feeling of calm. Whatever they do, if it helps them relax and think clearly, it is bound to improve their performance on the test.

Character Trait Analysis

Key Idea: The key idea is clearly stated in the first sentence.

Content: In the introductory paragraph the writer says that relaxing before a test has two aspects: mental and physical. The second paragraph is about relaxing mentally; the third is about relaxing physically. The examples in both paragraphs are clear; they are well-developed by details about selecting clothes, light exercise, and so on.

Organization: There are four well-constructed paragraphs in the essay. The first tells what the two middle paragraphs will be about. The middle paragraphs are each unified. The last paragraph presents concluding statements.

Conclusion or Summary: The conclusion could be stronger: it makes statements about other people's preparing for exams. It would have been better if the writer had left other people out, since that is not the subject of the essay.

Mechanics: There are no mechanical errors in the essay.

Practice Test 2

Directions: Refer to the GED Essay Scoring Guide (page 96) and the model essays that follow for help in evaluating your essay.

Model Essay—Holistic Score 3

States the point of view.

Develops one part of point of view, but in a confusing manner.

Develops other part of point of view, but in a confusing manner.

Restates point of view.

Air travel could be a good thing or a bad thing. Good because it means people can go more places and do more things. Thats always good. But bad because it means people move around more. It used to be that families stayed together in one place. You have to live close by because you knew that it would be hard to visit. Now its easier to visit, but it seems like people are moving around more and going further away. I don't think thats always such a good thing.

For people in business, air travel seems like a good thing because they can get to more customers. They don't have to spend days and days driving. Or if you need to talk to someone, you don't have to do it on the phone. You can fly right out and see them. But even for people in business, maybe it's not always such a good thing. Because then customers expect you to fly out. They would be hurt if you just called them up on the phone, when maybe you didn't really have time to fly. For me personally, I like that I can visit my grandchildren, but I don't like that they live so far away. I think there are good points and bad points to air travel.

Character Trait Analysis

Point of View: The key idea is not presented in one sentence, but in four. It is self-contradictory: the *good thing* is the same as the *bad thing.*

Content: Several different ideas come up in the two paragraphs of the essay: ideas about air travel and families, business people, and grandchildren. None of the ideas is clear; each seems self-contradictory. In the first paragraph, the writer never says directly how air travel is related to families' living apart. There are two ideas in the second paragraph: (1) air travel in business and (2) the writer's experience with air travel. One paragraph for each of those ideas could have been used to develop examples that would have made each support the point of view better.

Organization: The organization is poor. There is no clear introduction, middle, and conclusion. If there had been a clear point of view, then the two sides of air travel (good effects and bad effects) could have been discussed in separate paragraphs in the essay.

Conclusion or Summary: The last sentence is a restatement of the first sentence. No conclusion or summary follows.

Mechanics: There are many mechanical errors in this essay.

Model Essay—Holistic Score 5

States the point of view.

Air travel, like most of the benefits of technology, is a mixed blessing. Air travel has become such a part of modern life, however, that few people could imagine a world without planes, and few would want to.

Gives an example of a benefit of air travel.

Many air travelers are people in business. Salespeople looking for buyers, for example, used to be limited to the distances they could drive. For the cost of an airline ticket, they can now do business anywhere in the world.

Gives a second example of a benefit of air travel.

In the past, most people had only heard of places like the Bahamas or Hawaii. Many never even knew that places such as Tibet or Kenya exist. Now anyone who can afford the plane fare can actually explore these areas.

Gives a third example of a benefit of air travel.

Air travel influences even those who never set foot in an airplane. Many planes carry mail and freight. Packages that would have taken weeks or even months to reach their destinations now take only a few hours to arrive.

Gives examples of two problems associated with air travel.

As people who live near airports will tell you, there are problems associated with air travel. Airplanes contribute to both air and noise pollution. Because planes are bigger than ever, disasters, although rare, can take many lives. Hijackings also take place, and a few terrorists have used international air travel as a tool of violence.

Restates point of view and concludes.

Air travel has had an effect on everyone from the traveling salesperson to the person who has never left his home town. There is no doubt that it has caused some problems. The overall impact, however, has been to improve our lives and to give us a better idea of what the rest of the world is like.

Character Trait Analysis

Point of View: The key idea is clearly stated in the first sentence.

Content: There are five different examples, each in its own paragraph. The first three are examples of benefits of air travel; the fourth and fifth examples are problems associated with air travel. Each example is developed well with details.

Organization: The introductory paragraph would be improved if it flowed more clearly into the contents of the middle paragraphs by using words like *business, vac freight, accidents*, and *terrorists*. The middle paragraphs are each unified. The last paragraph restates the point of view and concludes.

Conclusion or Summary: The last paragraph is both a summary and a conclusion. It states that air travel is, overall, a benefit.

Mechanics: There are no mechanical errors in the essay.

Simulated Test, Part I

1. **(5)** *Sentence Structure/Parallelism/ Sentence Revision.* Express similar ideas in similar form. *You can look…, put in…, and receive….*

2. **(2)** *Usage/Subject–Verb Agreement/ Sentence Revision.* The singular subject, *shopping*, needs a singular verb, *requires*, despite the connective, *like*.

3. **(1)** *Mechanics/Punctuation/Comma Between Compound Sentences/Sentence Revision.* The comma belongs where it is placed before the connector, *but*. When two ideas that could each stand alone are joined with a connector such as *but, and, or,* or *for*, use a comma to separate the ideas.

4. **(5)** *Mechanics/Spelling/Homonyms/ Sentence Correction. Where* and *wear* sound somewhat alike but have different spellings.

5. **(1)** *Mechanics/Spelling/Homonyms/ Apostrophes/Contractions/Sentence Correction.* An apostrophe is needed in "It's" to make the contraction "It is." "Its" without an apostrophe is used to show possession.

6. **(1)** *Mechanics/Capitalization/Season/ Sentence Correction.* Seasons are not capitalized.

7. **(4)** *Sentence Structure/Parallelism/ Sentence Correction.* The sentence lists two things to do. Since the first thing to do is in command form, "add", the second thing to do should be in the same form. Therefore, change "remembering" to "remember."

8. **(3)** *Usage/Subject–Verb Agreement/ Either–Or/Sentence Correction.* When two singular nouns are connected by *either/or*, the subject is singular and requires a singular verb.

9. **(2)** *Usage/Pronoun Reference/ Construction Shift. Keep a record of your order, and check it right away upon delivery.* "It" refers to the order.

10. **(3)** *Sentence Structure/Improper Subordination/Sentence Correction.* When you make one part of a sentence dependent on another part, make sure that you use the correct relationship word.

11. **(2)** *Usage/Pronoun Reference/Agreement with Antecedent/Sentence Correction. His* does not agree with the word being replaced, *applicants*.

12. **(2)** *Mechanics/Punctuation/Comma after Introductory Words/Construction Shift. If you decide to answer a "help wanted" ad, select some plain stationery.* When an idea precedes the main part of a sentence, use a comma after the introductory idea.

13. **(3)** *Usage/Wrong Relative Pronoun/ Sentence Revision. Who* refers to people; *which* refers to things.

14. **(2)** *Usage/Pronoun Shift—Agreement with Antecedent/Sentence Correction.* When you address someone directly, use the pronoun *you. Your* (not *one's*) is in agreement with *you*.

15. **(1)** *Sentence Structure/Run-On/Sentence Correction.* Do not run together two ideas that each stand alone. Here, two separate sentences are formed to correct the run-on.

16. **(4)** *Sentence Structure/Subordination/ Construction Shift. Emphasize special achievements that are relevant to the position.* The new, more concise construction shows the relationship between the central and dependent ideas.

17. **(5)** *Mechanics/Punctuation/Comma After Introductory Words.* A comma should appear after *action* to show where the introduction ends.

18. **(2)** *Mechanics/Punctuation/Overuse of Comma/Sentence Revision.* The comma in this sentence is unnecessary, so omit it. A comma is used before "and" (1) to join two sentences or (2) if it separates items in a series.

19. **(3)** *Usage/Ambiguous Pronoun Reference/ Sentence Correction.* In the original sentence, *it* is ambiguous. It is not the postage or the envelope that is put in the mail, but the complete application.

20. **(3)** *Sentence Structure/Comma Splice/Sentence Correction.* Do not use a comma, alone, to separate two complete ideas. Here, the error is corrected by forming two sentences.

21. **(4)** *Mechanics/Capitalization/Proper Name–Place/Sentence Correction.* Capitalize *University* when it is part of the name of a particular school.

22. **(5)** *Usage/Subject–Verb Agreement– Inverted Structure/Sentence Correction.* The collective subject, *group* is considered singular and requires a singular verb, *was*, despite the fact that the usual subject/verb order is reversed.

23. **(5)** *Mechanics/Spelling/Frequently Misspelled Words—Rhythm/Sentence Correction.* Don't forget the silent *h* in *rhythm.*

24 **(4)** *Mechanics/Punctuation/Comma After Introduction/Sentence Correction.* A comma must be inserted after "selections" to show the reader where the introductory group of words ends.

25. **(5)** *Usage/Verb Tense—Word Clue to Tense in Paragraph/Sentence Revision.* The present tense is used throughout the paragraph.

26. **(2)** *Usage/Subject–Verb Agreement— Noun–Verb Pairs/Sentence Revision.* The plural subject, *Computers,* requires a plural verb, *are used.*

27. **(4)** *Sentence Structure/Dangling Modifier/ Sentence Revision.* It is not the *strange sounds,* but *anyone* who presses the keys. Keep the thing described as close as you can to its description.

28. **(3)** *Sentence Structure/Subordination/ Construction Shift. Computers have been used to write music that is consistent with the remaining pieces and also to improve the efficiency with which music is printed and stored.* No punctuation is used before "and" because the revised sentence is not compound.

29. **(5)** *Mechanics/Punctuation/Commas— Nonessential Phrase/Sentence Revision.* When a word or phrase comes directly after the word it describes, separate the two with a comma. Here, *a problem in getting to sleep or staying asleep* describes *insomnia* and should be separated from it by a comma.

30. **(2)** *Usage/Verb Tense/Word Clue to Tense Within Sentence/Sentence Correction.* The word *now* indicates that the present tense should be used:...there is now...

31. **(5)** *Mechanics/Capitalization/Proper Names/Sentence Correction.* The word *clinic* is left uncapitalized because here it is not part of the proper name of the clinic.

32. **(4)** *Sentence Structure/Parallelism/ Construction Shift. For most people with problems falling asleep or waking up too early, some simple remedies are often effective.* Use the "-ing" form of wake to be parallel with "falling."

33. **(3)** *Mechanics/Spelling/Troublesome Possessives/Sentence Correction.* Although many possessives are formed by adding *'s* there are exceptions, including *yours, theirs, his, hers,* and *its.*

34. **(3)** *Sentence Structure/Fragment/ Sentence Revision.* The main clause requires a subject and a verb to be complete. The implied subject is *you;* replacing *asking* with *ask* provides the verb.

35. **(5)** *Sentence Structure/Run-On/Sentence Revision.* Do not run together two complete ideas. Here, the connector *and* is used to correct the run-on by replacing *then.*

36. **(5)** *Usage/Pronoun Shift/Sentence Revision.* Don't shift pronouns mid-sentence.

37. **(5)** *Sentence Structure/Parallelism/ Sentence Correction.* Express similar ideas in similar form.... *it is probably better to turn...than to lie...*

38. **(5)** *Sentence Structure/Run-on/Sentence Revision.* Use a semicolon to connect two sentences that are joined by connectors such as *thus, therefore,* and *however.*

39. **(1)** *Usage/Subject–Verb Agreement— Interrupting Phrase/Sentence Revision.* The singular subject, *One,* requires a singular verb, *is,* despite the interrupting phrase, *of the main reasons.*

40. **(3)** *Mechanics/Capitalization/Dates— Holidays/Sentence Correction.* Only the names of particular holidays are capitalized.

41. **(3)** *Sentence Structure/Fragment/ Sentence Correction.* When a sentence contains an "ing" word, make sure there is a verb for the subject. The singular subject, *reason,* requires a singular verb, *is.*

42. **(1)** *Usage/Relative Pronoun/Sentence Correction. Which* refers to things and *who* refers to people.

43. **(2)** *Usage/Subject–Verb Agreement— Noun–Verb Pairs/Construction Shift. When someone wants to moonlight, he needs to find out how his present employer feels about second jobs.* The singular subject, *someone,* requires a singular verb, *wants.*

44. **(5)** *Sentence Structure/Improper Subordination/Sentence Revision.* When making one part of a sentence dependent on another, don't use more than one relationship word....*a line stating that....*

45. **(2)** *Usage/Subject–Verb Agreement— Expletives/Sentence Revision.* The subject is not *There* or *reasons,* but the singular *one,* which requires a singular verb, *is.*

46. **(5)** *Sentence Structure/Subordination/ Construction Shift.* The employer may be concerned about the employee's doing extra work and being too tired to function efficiently on his full-time job. Needless repetition is avoided.

47. **(2)** *Mechanics/Punctuation/Apostrophe/ Contractions/Sentence Correction.* The apostrophe in contractions stands for the missing letter or letters: *isn't* stands for *is not*.

48. **(4)** *Sentence Structure/Fragment/ Sentence Revision.* The singular subject, *Football*, requires a singular verb, *has changed*.

49. **(1)** *Usage/Subject–Verb Agreement— Noun–Verb Pairs/Sentence Correction.* The plural subject, *rules*, requires a plural verb, *bear*.

50. **(3)** *Usage/Verb Tense/Sentence Revision.* The past tense must be used in this sentence because the previous sentence is written in the past and this sentence uses *For many years* to indicate past tense. A singular verb form is used to agree with the singular subject *football*.

51. **(5)** *Sentence Structure/Subordination/ Sentence Correction.* When you use *so/that* or *such/that* to make one part of a sentence dependent on another, be sure to include both of the relationship words.

52. **(4)** *Usage/Verb Tense/Sentence Revision.* The verb "decided" indicates past tense. The comma is used after "saw" to indicate the ending of an introductory phrase.

53. **(4)** *Mechanics/Capitalization/Places/ States/Sentence Correction.* Capitalize the proper names of places such as states, nations, and continents.

54. **(3)** *Mechanics/Punctuation/Comma Between Items in a Series/Sentence Correction.* Use commas to separate three or more items in a series.

55. **(5)** *Sentence Structure/Clarity/ Construction Shift. In New Brunswick you will find the headquarters of the National Football Foundation and Hall of Fame.* By beginning with *In New Brunswick,* you don't need the awkward phrase, *if you go to New Brunswick.*

Simulated Test, Part II

Directions: Refer to the GED Essay Scoring Guide (page 96) and the model essays that follow for help in evaluating your essay.

Model Essay—Holistic Score 3

States the point of view poorly.

Its not right to tell people they can't smoke in public. Thats what public means—that its for people. If people don't want you to smoke in their house, OK. That's their right. But how can somebody tell me not to smoke in public? I'm part of the public, aren't I? So I should be able to smoke. Besides, I always try to watch out for the other guy. If I think my smoke is bothering somebody, I ask them. If they tell me, I put out my cigarette. Can't other people do this too? Do they need a law to regulate every little thing? There are too many laws allready anyway. This is a personal problem. It shouldn't be handled by law. It should be handled between people.

Lists two reasons to support point of view, but does not develop them well.

Lists a third reason.

Some people are worried about their health. If they have asthma, or if they are pregnant. Or allergic to smoke. All right, then they should say something. But there are lots of things that could make them sick. Like cars and trucks and other pollution. Smoking is only a little part of what could make them sick. So why pick on smokers? I think that people should be able to do what they want in public, including smoking.

Restates point of view, again poorly.

Character Trait Analysis

Key Idea: The key idea is presented in the first sentence of the essay, but it is poorly stated. The writer allows individuals to ask a smoker to put a cigarette out, but thinks the legal system should not have that right. That distinction is not made clear in the first sentence.

Content: The writer introduces three different reasons for opposing legal restrictions on smoking in public. The reasons are not developed well enough to make the writer's point of view clear, however. The sentence "There are too many laws allready anyway" does not explain *why* the legal system should not handle restrictions on smoking in public places. The writer could have explained the point of view more fully: for example, *Because most smokers are courteous and thoughtful, they would be happy to stop smoking in public if someone asked them to. Therefore, a law is not necessary. A law would be difficult and expensive to enforce. Why have a law that is unnecessary?*

Organization: There is no introductory or concluding paragraph. The whole essay is presented in two paragraphs, neither of which is unified. The first paragraph contains two ideas: that there should be no restrictions on smoking in public, and that the legal system should not regulate smoking. The second paragraph argues that smoking is a relatively minor problem in the face of other kinds of pollution. If each of those reasons had been stated directly in a topic sentence and developed in its own paragraph, the organization would have been much more effective.

Conclusion or Summary: The last sentence restates the idea in the first sentence. It is not a good conclusion of the essay because it does not bring up the difference between regulation by law and the kind of regulation smokers are willing to impose on themselves—which is the point of the essay.

Mechanics: There are many sentence fragments and other mechanical errors in the essay that further weaken its effectiveness.

Model Essay—Holistic Score 5

States point of view in one sentence.

Gives one reason for banning smoking.

Argues against measures less strict than banning smoking.

Gives examples of health problems associated with smoking.

Restates point of view and concludes.

Smoking should be banned in all public places, because few people argue any longer about whether or not smoking is a health hazard.

One person's freedom to smoke should not be allowed to violate someone else's freedom to breathe clean air. Smoke poses an immediate health threat to people with problems such as asthma. Studies have shown that smoke-filled air can be harmful to the rest of us, too, because it increases our risk of developing lung cancer.

While the idea of providing both smoking and nonsmoking areas sounds like a fair solution, in reality it does not work very well. My experience has been that ventilation on planes, in restaurants, and elsewhere is inadequate to prevent smoke from drifting from the smoking to the nonsmoking areas.

There are good reasons to ban smoking altogether in public. Numerous studies show that cigarettes contribute to health problems: smoking is linked to lung cancer, high blood pressure, and low birthweights of babies of smokers. People who must inhale others' smoke in public places are at risk even though they choose not to smoke.

In summary, protecting people's health is a sound reason for banning smoking in all public areas. I respect the right of adults to smoke in their own homes, but I think the law should protect my right to breathe clean air.

Character Trait Analysis

Key Idea: The key idea, that smoking should be banned, is stated in one sentence in the introductory paragraph at the beginning of the essay.

Content: The essay presents three supporting ideas in three separate paragraphs: (1) nonsmokers deserve clean air, (2) nonsmoking areas do not assure nonsmokers clean air, and (3) health risks to nonsmokers are reason enough to ban smoking in public altogether. Each idea is supported by one example or more.

Organization: There is an introductory and concluding paragraph. Each of the three mid paragraphs is unified and presents an idea that supports the key idea.

Conclusion or Summary: The last paragraph restates the point of view and concludes that nonsmokers have the right to breathe clean air.

Mechanics: There are few mechanical errors in the essay.